BUSINESS WRITING BASICS

BUSINESS WRITING BASICS

Jane Watson

Self-Counsel Press
(a division of)
International Self-Counsel Press Ltd.
USA   Canada

Self-Counsel Press acknowledges the financial support of the Government of Canada through the Book Publishing Industry Development Program (BPIDP) for our publishing activities.

Printed in Canada.
First edition: 1996; Reprinted: 1996; 1998
Second edition: 2002
Third edition: 2007

Library and Archives Canada Cataloguing in Publication

Watson, Jane, 1948–
    Business writing basics / Jane Watson. — 3rd ed.

ISBN 978-1-55180-769-0

    1. Business writing. 2. English language—Business English.
I. Title.
HF5718.3.W37 2007   808'.066651   C2007-900458-X

Self-Counsel Press
(a division of)
International Self-Counsel Press Ltd.

1704 North State Street	1481 Charlotte Road
Bellingham, WA 98225	North Vancouver, BC V7J 1H1
USA	Canada

This book is dedicated to my best friend and husband, Colin, and to my wonderful support staff: children — John, Timothy, and Suzanne — and mother, Mary Thomas.

CONTENTS

SAMPLES

WORKSHEETS

TABLES

CHECKLISTS

PREFACE

Years ago when I decided to become a professional trainer in the field of business writing, I did so with the thought that there seemed to be a small, consistent need for information in this area, and that I could fill it while balancing work and home.

This plan would certainly have surprised my high school teachers and university professors who had to deal with my misguided attempts to put my thoughts on paper. Writing was an area I dreaded. Ironically, my first job was in communications and required the writing of news releases, articles, and briefing notes. With the help and patience of my manager and colleagues, I developed a clear business writing style. In fact, I soon learned to love organizing ideas in a written format.

When my children came along, it made sense for me to work part time, and offering workshops in business writing was a perfect fit.

After doing this for a number of months, I found that at the end of a session, participants often asked where they could get more information to stay on track in improving their writing. After all, in a one- or two-day workshop, you cannot possibly learn all the tips that can make a major difference in your writing style. However, I could not locate an easy-to-read, high-content book to recommend.

We all have busy lives. I wanted a book that someone could pick up at any page and quickly get a tip that would help them — hence, *Business Writing Basics* (originally called *Write On!: Business Writing Basics*). Although it would be useful, there is no need to read the book from cover to cover.

This is the third edition of *Business Writing Basics,* and it is interesting to note the changes that have occurred over the past few years in both my business life and in the book. From conducting a few workshops a month, I now deliver over 100 days of training a year across the country and have become involved in personalized coaching for senior executives.

The content of the book has also grown. Initially, it focused on writing clearly and concisely and on business correspondence. The second edition included material on email messages and a chapter on writing for the World Wide Web.

This version strengthens the email section and also provides information on PowerPoint slides and on business case studies — increasingly important tools today.

I hope that by reading this book, you'll share my enjoyment of the world of writing and pick up suggestions to help you become a more powerful communicator when using the written word.

Chapter 1

BUSINESS WRITING — THERE HAVE BEEN SOME CHANGES

As a trainer and consultant in business writing for almost two decades, I have seen a number of things changing in the field as well as a number of things staying the same.

What has stayed the same? The three ingredients for successful writing — whether you are writing a letter, an email, a report, or a business case — remain the same:

- A strong reader focus
- A clear, concise writing style
- Attention to grammar and spelling

What has changed is the addition of three more areas now considered essential for effective writing:

- A strong organizational pattern
- A tone that is appropriate for the reader and the message
- A visually appealing page

Let's look at all these areas in more detail.

READER FOCUS

This is still an important concept that many writers fail to grasp. Everyone knows the adage "write to the reader." However, many give it lip service. They claim that they adjust their messages to the reader, but they often fail. They get too excited about what interests them personally, or by areas that have taken them a long time to research. They emphasize the wrong points and fail to answer readers' questions.

In addition, I believe many business writers are not sure who today's readers really are. Generally, business readers are busy, overworked, stressed, overly sensitive, easily distracted, and overwhelmed with the amount of reading they have to do. As a result, they skim documents, get their feelings hurt when they believe a message is too abrupt or dictatorial, and lose their focus when they see spelling or grammar errors.

All successful business documents are the ones that answer the reader's questions. Readers live by the law of easiest decision. If they are quickly able to obtain the information they need, they are more likely to take positive action. If they feel the need to think about your request, or they think they need more details, or — worse still — they believe they should refer the document to a committee for more investigation, you will rarely get the response you want.

CLEAR, CONCISE WRITING

Over the years, people have finally begun to recognize that clarity and conciseness are the way to go in business writing. The number of workshop participants who fight me on this has diminished greatly.

Writers are finally becoming aware that long, complicated sentences and a reliance on outdated expressions are no longer considered professional in the business world. Whether a reader is high on the corporate ladder or nearer to the bottom, he or she wants and needs a document that can be read and understood quickly. In today's business world, no one has the time to try to interpret another's message.

GRAMMAR AND SPELLING

This is a strange area. When asked, writers often tell me that spelling and grammar are not as important as they once were. However, upon reflection they usually change their minds and give examples of their pet peeves when reading other people's messages.

In other words, spelling and grammar matter to readers, not to writers. To me, poor spelling and faulty grammar are like having bad breath. Few people will tell you directly that it bothers them, but it sure stands out. And it is a sure way to ruin a professional image.

Too often writers depend solely on their computer software packages to point out errors. Be careful. Software packages are a mixed blessing. Nowadays, you can use your computers to check spelling, grammar, and readability levels. However, you can't rely on software exclusively. Documents must still be proofread manually as well as electronically because spell checkers don't always catch words that are spelled correctly but are misused, such as *its* versus *it's* and *deer* instead of *dear.*

Similarly, they don't point out all grammar errors, as the computer cannot determine what you actually meant to say. They may even draw your attention to punctuation or phrases that are correct. It is up to you to make the final decision.

In addition, grammar packages can indicate errors, and readability indexes can point out the difficulty of the reading level of your documents, but the packages don't provide enough information on how to fix the problems they catch. It is up to you to look up any grammar or style points you don't understand — check your grammar book or speak with your English guru. Don't ignore the problem just because you don't understand it. The software package has pointed it out for a reason.

ORGANIZATION

Organization is an area that is gaining more and more importance in business writing. In fact, I would say it is being given even more emphasis than clarity and conciseness. I am now getting calls asking for business writing workshops that don't focus on the writing aspect at all. The required emphasis is on the arrangement of ideas.

Today's readers tend to want the bottom line first, and then the supporting details. They want to know in the opening paragraph why they should spend their valuable time on your document. They also want to see how the ideas relate to each other. And they don't want to hunt for the answers to their questions.

TONE

Tone is another area that is gaining in importance, particularly when sending emails. In the past, writers used very formal words and phrases. This was the normal language of the day. People tended to — and were expected to — speak formally. If you use these same words and tone in talking with a client or customer today, you are regarded as dated and pompous.

The same is true for your writing. Whether you are communicating internally with staff or externally with customers, you should write in a friendly, courteous fashion, using the same words and tone you would use if you were meeting the reader face to face.

Tell the reader what you can do, rather than what you can't. If you are listing features, include benefits. Use the active voice. Include the reader's name. And use words that are common to your normal conversation. For example, I doubt that if a human resources person would ever say, "A prompt reply will expedite consideration of the student's application." If you wouldn't say it, don't write it.

Today, write as though you are speaking — assuming you speak in a grammatically correct fashion.

VISUAL APPEAL

In the past, the look of a written document would not normally be connected to business writing. However, I now place a great deal of emphasis on this area. Why?

Business readers are extremely busy, and they are easily intimidated. If they receive a print or screen document that looks difficult to digest, they put it aside until later — and later seldom comes.

If you don't focus on the visual appeal of your message, your readers may not get around to reading it. They may not take the time to discover that you have written clear, concise sentences, that your thoughts are organized, that your spelling and grammar are perfect, and that your tone is correct.

IN SUMMARY

Reader focus, clarity and conciseness, and good grammar and spelling have always been characteristics of effective business writing. Over the last decade, we have added organization, tone, and visual appeal. These three additional concepts are essential in meeting the reading needs of today's business people.

The following chapters are designed to provide you with practical guidelines for incorporating these characteristics into your letters, emails, reports, and business cases.

Chapter 2

13 WAYS TO MIND YOUR READER'S BUSINESS AND PUT YOUR OWN ON THE BACK BURNER

One of the main changes in business writing over the recent years has been in terms of writers' focus. Even until the end of the last century, writers tended to write about what they knew and what they wanted the reader to know. Now effective writers "speak" about what the reader wants to know and needs to know. This change in focus from the sender's interests to the receiver's needs means that writers must understand their readers before they begin to write.

In one of my workshops, a young man firmly opposed this idea. He was "much too busy to consider the reader" before he composed an email message or letter. It was a waste of his time. Yet this same person also admitted his readers didn't always follow through the way he wanted. Nor was it unusual for him to receive phone calls or emails requesting additional information, and sometimes he had to write a second letter to clarify the first. His manager claimed the young man produced dull, lifeless material that often rambled or irritated readers.

Vague ideas, irrelevant details, missing information, inappropriate tone, boring delivery — these are some of the things that can detract from your message if you fail to think about your reader before you write.

There is a marvelous saying that applies both to report and correspondence writing: "Typists pound keyboards, and writers stare out windows." In other words, if you busy yourself on your keyboard before you are clear about your reader and the reason for writing, consider yourself a typist. However, if you sit back and think before you begin to input your ideas, you will be an effective writer. And if you learn to see through your readers' eyes, talk their language, and present the message in a manner that will appeal to them, then your correspondence will develop an interesting, helpful personality.

Undoubtedly, there are occasions when you don't know much about your reader. If you are answering a letter or email from a stranger or responding to a quick phone call, you will have to generalize. But the more you focus on your reader, the better your correspondence will be.

Here are some questions to ask yourself about your readers before you begin to write:

1. What is the vocabulary level of your readers? Is English their main language? Are they comfortable with long, complicated words, or are simpler words better? In addition, although long-time residents of a country may know numerous words for an item, new arrivals may know only one.

2. How much education do the readers have? Do they have a general education or are they specialists in the same field as you? Is it appropriate to use jargon or "insider" words?

3. What is the approximate age of the readers? Are they in the workforce? Although older readers may prefer a more formal tone, they still may want clear, concise documents.

   Many business people are becoming older and reaching the point where they require reading glasses. Ensure your typeface is a reasonable size.

4. How are you related to the reader? Are you writing to your boss, the public, a client, a potential customer, the president of your company, or the board of directors? Your tone must change accordingly. Generally, emails to your boss and colleagues are less formal than letters written to clients.

5. What do your readers do for a living? How much understanding do they have of this particular subject? Conveying information of a legal nature to a lawyer requires different words than conveying the same information to a layperson.

6. How many times have you written to these readers about this topic? Is this the first time, so that background details are needed? Is this the second, third, or fourth time you've written? If so, reduce or eliminate the background and concentrate on the current details.

7. What special interests or concerns will the readers have regarding this information? Are you writing a report for politicians whose constituents are affected by your message? If so, you had better include a strong analysis of the pros and cons of your message. Are you writing a proposal to people who believe another company should be the chosen vendor? You will need some strong arguments and some creative thinking to convince them otherwise.

8. Are there any economic or staff constraints that will be foremost in the readers' minds when they read your material? If you are recommending spending money your organization doesn't have, you may be wasting your time with this correspondence, or you may have to be particularly persuasive and explain where the money can be found.

9. What sort of reports do the readers normally want to receive? If you know they prefer reports of no more than two pages in length, don't give them a ten-page document. If you know they want the recommendation at the top of the first page, that's where you should put it.

10. If your readers are in a different country, their writing rules may differ. It is not only courteous but also good business sense to try to adapt your writing style to theirs.

    The British have a much more formal writing style and tend to use expressions North Americans consider outdated. The British consider the North American "natural" tone disrespectful. Japanese writers are extremely polite and begin letters with references to impersonal topics, such as the weather. Their writing style is indirect, as opposed to the North American desire for clarity and conciseness. In reports, the Japanese tend to present information in chronological order. German reports include detailed background information whether readers require it or not. The tradition in France is to begin reports with the theory behind the problem and follow with the history. Writers from Latin countries often subscribe to the theory "more is best," and include numerous details and adjectives. They tend to play down bad news.

    Stay alert to the different meanings of words. Although English, Spanish, Portuguese, French, and Italian are all based on Latin, they developed differently. Therefore, some words have a different range of meanings according to the country. For example, the French word for teacher is *le professeur*. However, in English the term *professor* is used only for a teacher at a university.

11. What do the readers need to know about this topic in order to take action? And what do they want to know? As soon as you have focused on this information, you can eliminate all other details.

12. How do you want your readers to react to your message? Do you want them to take some action? In that case, your request should be concrete, concise, and direct. If the information is bad news, you will want to maintain their goodwill and future cooperation. This affects the organization of the message.

Do you want them to feel some emotion? Do you want them excited about your idea or your product so they will want it, or do you need them to be concerned so they'll contribute to your charity? This information alters your word choice.

13. Are there any secondary readers? Secondary readers are people to whom a copy of your correspondence is given. For example, if your boss is pleased with the report you have written, he or she may pass it on to a manager. That manager is your second reader, and the report should be written and organized in a manner that will meet his or her needs.

Worksheet 1 is a planning tool for analyzing your reader. If you use it before you begin to write, you will find that, in the long run, you will produce reports and correspondence more efficiently. In addition, you will start getting the response you want from your readers, as you will be writing more clearly, with the appropriate tone.

WORKSHEET 1
PLANNING TOOL FOR READER ANALYSIS

	PRIMARY READER		
Reader's background			
Relationship to writer			
Vocabulary level	*Basic*	*Standard*	*Technical*
Tone	*Informal*	*Neutral*	*Formal*
Information reader already has			
Details the reader needs to know			
Details the reader wants to know			
Reader's reaction	*Pleased*	*Upset*	*Indifferent*
Action you want reader to take			

Are there any secondary readers?

Chapter 3

38 PRACTICAL WRITING TIPS YOU NEVER LEARNED IN SCHOOL

Although writing ranks as one of the key skills needed in business today, few people have received extensive training in this area. They have either specialized in courses that require little writing, such as mathematics, or they have taken courses that concentrate on academic writing, which is not the same as business writing.

Academic writing differs from business writing primarily in terms of the reader and the goal. In academic writing, the writer is trying to convince a limited audience that he or she knows a great deal about a specific topic. The reader is usually an expert in the field and is paid to read and to critique the document.

In the business world, documents are usually written for multiple readers who may not be familiar with the subject matter. Business documents are prepared under time and money constraints. In addition, the readers don't have to — or don't wish to — take the time to sort through and interpret long, complicated messages. Therefore, today's business communications require a style of writing that is concise, clear, and easy to read.

This chapter is devoted to specific, easily adopted tips that ensure your correspondence — whether it travels by "snail mail" or by electronic methods — meets the needs of the marketplace and projects an image of you as a professional, customer-oriented, clear-thinking individual.

THE READER

1. **Knowing your reader is the key to success.** The number one rule of all communications — written or spoken — is to know your audience. Everything hinges on this information. It is so important, I devoted a whole chapter to it. If you have not yet read Chapter 2, I suggest you go back and do so.

WORD CHOICE

2. **Simple words work best.** Reading comprehension studies show that people absorb information faster if it is written slightly below their normal comprehension levels. And if they are in business — whether they are on their own or working for someone else — they don't have time to check a dictionary or ponder the meanings of unfamiliar words.

   Although there are over a million words in the English language, the average adult has a working vocabulary of only 5,000 words and learns just two new words a year. In addition, most of the words in the English language have more than one meaning.

   To ensure the average reader interprets your message correctly, choose short, simple words. This will reduce the chance for misunderstandings. Table 1 shows a list of words that have been standard fare in business correspondence and offers you some alternative, simpler words to use in their place.

   Some readers may ask what will happen to the English language if we eliminate the fancy words. But polysyllabic words are still available for creative or recreational writing.

3. **Jargon has its place.** Jargon is the technical language used by a specific group or profession. If you're writing for such a group, jargon can explain concepts more clearly

TABLE 1
EASIER-TO-READ WORDS

INSTEAD OF	USE
alleviate	lessen, ease
ameliorate	improve
anticipate	expect
ascertain	determine, find out
as per your request	as you requested
cognizant	aware
consequence	result, outcome
despite the fact that	although
enable	allow, help
endeavor	try
eventuality	result, outcome
expedite	speed up
facilitate	help, aid
forward	send
immediately	now, right away
implement	start
initiate	start, begin
in order to	to
necessitates	requires
notwithstanding	but, despite, regardless
occurrence	event, incident
perusal	review, information
signify	mean
substantiate	support, prove
under no circumstances	never
utilize	use
variation	change
whether or not	if

and concisely than plain English, and it helps build rapport with a technical reader. For example, the word *iterative* is quite common with engineers, but is confusing to most other people. Likewise, *efficacy* is familiar to health-care professionals but leaves others shaking their heads.

Use jargon when you know the word is appropriate for the intended audience. Otherwise, a breakdown in communications could occur.

4. **Each word you write should have a purpose.** Good business writing is economical. Every word is included for a reason: to convey a message, set a tone, or connect ideas. This means all unnecessary words should be eliminated. If two words mean nearly the same thing, the less expressive one should go.

    Example   In addition, we are also sending you our latest brochure.

    Better   In addition, we are sending you our latest brochure.

    Example   In my past experience ... (*How many experiences have you had that weren't in your past?*)

    Better   In my experience ...

    Example   First and foremost

    Better   First

    The word *that* is often overused. Whenever you find yourself writing it, read the sentence aloud to determine if you really need it. Most of the time, the sentence reads better without it.

    Example   I understand that you are looking for a new account manager.

    Better   I understand you need a new account manager.

5. **Intensive words, such as *very, highly, greatly,* and *extremely,* detract from your professional image.** Intensives should be used with care. They lean toward

overstatement, which may cause the reader to doubt your reliability. They also imply information that cannot be measured, as everyone gives the words his or her own subjective meaning.

Example   I was very pleased to talk with you last week regarding ...

Better   I was pleased to talk with you last week regarding ...

6. **Connecting words or phrases will help you "drive" your reader through your material.** Words such as *however, in addition,* and *to summarize* signal the reader that the upcoming statement supports (green light), conflicts with (red light), or illustrates (yellow light) the preceding point. Table 2 lists some connecting words you can use to move your writing along in different situations.

   If you don't use connecting words, your writing will appear disjointed. Readers will be forced to interpret it themselves; they may even give up and turn to easier-to-read material.

   I recommend a connecting word or phrase approximately every third sentence. I have yet to find anyone who overuses this technique.

   Note: Sentences may begin with *and* or *but*. Although this practice was frowned upon years ago, these words serve as excellent connectors in emails and some letters. They make it sound as if we are talking to our reader; therefore, it is now acceptable to use them.

   For more formal documents, you would use *in addition* and *however*.

7. **Clichés are boring.** Clichés are words and phrases that were refreshing in bygone years. Now they are meaningless. You might get away with the occasional cliché, but too many will give your correspondence a stilted, insincere tone. Table 3 lists common clichés and their modern replacements.

TABLE 2
CONNECTING WORDS AND PHRASES

PURPOSE	FORMAL	INFORMAL
Comparison	similarly, in comparison	again, likewise, still
Time	eventually, formerly, subsequently	then, next, after, later, since, while
Same direction	furthermore, moreover, in addition	and, first, second, third, besides, also
Contrast	however, nevertheless, on the contrary	but, still, yet, meanwhile, on the other hand
Illustration	to illustrate, in other words	for example
Conclusion	therefore, accordingly, in conclusion	so, as a result, to sum up, in short
Emphasis	in any event, to be sure	of course, naturally, obviously

TABLE 3
CLICHÉS TO AVOID

CLICHÉ	REPLACEMENT
At your earliest convenience, At an early date, At this time	*If you have a date, give it.*
At this writing, At this point in time	*If you mean now, say "now."*
Attached please find Please find enclosed Enclosed please find You will find	Attached is/are Enclosed is/are Enclosed is/are Here is/are
Hereto/herewith/hereby/ said/above/same/thereof/ wherein/hereinafter	*These words are legalese. Delete them.*
I remain	*Old-fashioned — delete*
Permit me to say	*Useless filler — delete*
I would like to take this opportunity to	*Useless filler — delete*
This letter is for the purpose of	*Useless filler — delete*
We wish to acknowledge receipt of	We have received
As per your request, Pursuant to your request, Referring to your request, In reference to your letter	As requested, As you requested in your letter of May 3, In response to
The writer, The undersigned	Me, I
Thanking you in advance	Thank you for …
Under separate cover	Separately

8. **Strong verbs create powerful messages.** Many writers unconsciously take strong verbs and turn them into nouns. Then they search for another verb to fit the sentence. Not only does this rob sentences of their strength and vitality, but it adds additional, unnecessary words.

To remedy this problem, go over your writing and "flag" all words ending with *-ance*, *-ment*, and *-ion*. Whenever possible, replace these words with a verb.

Example   This letter is a confirmation of the details of our meeting last Tuesday.

Better   This letter confirms the details of last Tuesday's meeting.

Example   Preparation of an agenda should be done before a meeting.

Better   Prepare an agenda before the meeting.

9. **Helping verbs aren't always helpful.** There is a category of verbs called helping verbs. They help other verbs express their meanings. However, they can weaken a message. Whenever possible, replace them with strong action verbs.

Helping verbs include:

- Be (am, is, are, was, were, been)
- Have (has, had)
- Do (does, did)
- Shall
- Should
- Would

Example   I will have (*helping verbs*) completed the project by Friday.

Better   I will complete the project by Friday.

Example   I have been (*helping verbs*) invited to tour the plant.

Better   I am invited to tour the plant.

Note: Eliminating all helping verbs is impossible. But every time you delete or replace one, your sentence becomes stronger.

10. **Verbs and phrases should inspire confidence.** *Would, might,* and *could* are weak verbs. Delete them, or replace them with the more positive words *will* and *can.*

Example	Would you please send us a copy of the financial statement?
Better	Will you please send us a copy of the financial statement?
Better	Please send us a copy of the financial statement.

11. **Impersonal phrases weaken ideas.** Impersonal phrases such as *it was suggested, it seems, it appears, we should consider, we seem to be in favor,* and *it may be that* ... are too tentative. Whenever you use these wimpy phrases, you lose credibility. Eliminate them.

Example	It appears the figures are inaccurate.
Better	The figures are inaccurate.

12. **Be careful when using abbreviations.** Abbreviations are shortened forms of words. They may consist of the first few letters, such as *Nov.* for *November,* or just the consonants, *amt.* for *amount.* Abbreviations are fine for emails, tables, and graphs. They are not recommended for letters or reports as they make the writer look lazy. Take the time to write the words in full, and give yourself the image of an energetic professional. Avoid *etc.* (except in emails).

Example	At our next meeting, we will discuss forecasting, customer surveys, new leads, etc.
Better	At our next meeting, some of the items we will discuss are forecasting, customer suveys, and new leads.
Better	At our next meeting, some of the items we will discuss are:

    - Forecasting

- Customer surveys
- New leads

13. **Initial letters of words can form abbreviations.** For example, *Credit Valley Hospital* becomes *CVH*. Too many abbreviations of this type make readers feel they are looking at a bowl of alphabet soup. If you do need the occasional acronym for faster reading, make sure you define it the first time you use it.

   Example   Credit Valley Hospital (CVH) is known for its commitment to community involvement. Staff from CVH regularly volunteer at the food bank.

   Note: If more than five pages have passed since you spelled out an acronym or abbreviation, the reader may have forgotten what it stands for. You should redefine it.

14. **Contractions give writing an informal tone.** Contractions are words that have been shortened by omitting letters, for example, *it's* instead of *it is* or *can't* instead of *cannot*. Use contractions in email messages or in informal letters. When writing a report, all words should be spelled out — avoid contractions.

SENTENCES

15. **The first and last words of a sentence stand out.** People read the same way they watch a situation comedy on TV. They turn on in the beginning, tune out in the middle, come back for the end, and assume they understand what went on. Be careful you don't bury crucial information in the middle of a long sentence. It may get overlooked.

   Example   In the near future, sales will be hiring two new account managers as we work on improving our customer service. (*"In the near future" stands out, as does "improving our customer service."*)

   Better   Two new account managers, who will be hired by sales in the near future, will help us improve customer service. (*"Two new account managers" and "improve customer service" are now the key points.*)

16. **The average length of a sentence in business writing is 15–18 words.** This is the easiest length for a reader to absorb quickly.

17. **Sentences over 18 words irritate readers**. The reader will either skip over details or interpret the message incorrectly. Break long sentences into two or three shorter ones.

    Example   Our intent in forwarding the list of priority short-term capital projects in advance of the final report has been to fast-track the approval process in anticipation of a review of each capital project to be conducted by government staff with your staff.

    Better   Attached is the list of priority short-term capital projects. We are sending you this information before the final report is released to fast-track the approval process. This early release of the information should help your staff be prepared when the anticipated government review occurs.

18. **The best correspondence includes a variety of sentence lengths.** Too many long sentences are confusing. Too many short sentences read like baby talk. A variety of lengths appeals to readers.

19. **Sentences requiring more than four pieces of punctuation are hard to read.** A sentence that includes so many details it requires this much punctuation will be difficult for your reader to digest. Break it into two or more sentences. (Don't forget to include the period or question mark at the end of the sentence as part of your punctuation count.)

    Example   In addition, I would recommend the board make a priority of a five-year planning document, which is scheduled to be presented, as part of its annual review process, to senior management in the first week of March.

Better   In addition, I recommend the department make the preparation of a five-year planning document a priority. The document is scheduled for presentation to senior management in March as part of the annual review process.

Note: This technique will also help you present your points in a logical, easy-to-read manner.

20. **Lists are the best way to convey three or more points.** Point-form lists help the reader absorb information, and they provide white space. (See Rule 28.)

Example   There are three possible solutions under the present legislation: use only the locations accessible to the handicapped, renovate poorly designed locations, or install temporary ramps.

Better   There are three possible solutions under the present legislation:

- Use only the locations accessible to the handicapped.
- Renovate poorly designed locations.
- Install temporary ramps.

Note: Use punctuation with lists if the points are expressed in complete sentences or long phrases (as in the example above). No periods are required — even after the final item — if the list is made up of sentence fragments. (See example in Rule 12.)

Capitalizing the first letter of each point is optional, but be consistent with your choice.

You can use numbers, letters, or dashes (—) instead of bullets (•); however, numbers and letters may give your readers the impression that the first point deserves more attention than the last. If points are listed in order of importance, use numbers.

Don't forget to indent your lists so they stand out on the page.

21. **Good news should be placed in a short sentence, preferably in a short paragraph.** Good news stands out more clearly if it is in a short, easy-to-read sentence.

> **Example** This year, after a careful fine-tuning of our budget, we were able to reduce our administrative costs by a grand total of $300,000.
>
> **Better** This year we saved $300,000 in administrative costs.

22. **Bad news should never be delivered in a short sentence, unless you are deliberately trying to upset a reader.** Soften bad news by putting it in a longer sentence and defusing the message.

> **Example** The report will be a week late.
>
> **Better** The report will be a week late, but it will include the latest figures.
>
> **Example** The repairs will cost $12,000.
>
> **Better** Although the repairs will cost $12,000, additional work will not be required for two years.

23. **Active voice sentences are preferable, but don't throw out all passive voice sentences.** Voice is a grammatical term referring to the relationship between a subject and verb in a sentence. In the active voice, the person or thing that is the subject is doing the acting and appears at the beginning of the sentence. In other words, active voice sentences state who did what. In the passive voice, often called backward writing, the subject is being acted upon and often appears at the end of the sentence or is missing. Passive voice sentences say what was done or what was done by whom.

> **Examples** Suzanne Watson handled the customer's complaint. (*Active voice/who did what*)

The customer's complaint was handled by Suzanne Watson. (*Passive voice/what was done by whom*)

Use Form 2-11 to record any variations in standard procedures. (*Active voice/who should do what — the "you" is understood*)

Any variations in standard procedures should be recorded on Form 2-11. (*Passive voice/what was done*)

Accomplished business writers make a conscious decision when to use the passive voice because it —

(a) uses more words,

(b) is not as direct as the active voice, and

(c) gives your writing a more formal tone.

On the other hand, don't eliminate the passive voice entirely. It is ideal for presenting negative findings in a report or for pointing out a problem when you don't want to place specific blame. Technical reports and formal minutes are often written in the passive voice because "the what" is more important than "the who."

Example   You should not make critical remarks in public. (*Active voice/who did what*)

Example   Critical remarks should not be made in public. (*Passive voice/what was done*)

PARAGRAPHS

24. **Opening and closing paragraphs in letters, memos, and reports should not be more than three to four lines long.** Business writing is psychological. If your opening paragraphs are too long, they will discourage your readers from taking the time to continue reading. Sample 1 shows a letter with a long opening paragraph. In Sample 2, this paragraph has been broken into three parts. The

opening paragraph is shorter, and the subhead provides more white space.

Closing paragraphs should also be brief, and they should clearly indicate the action the reader is to take. If this information is conveyed clearly and concisely, you are more likely to get the results you want.

25. **Paragraphs in the body of a letter, memo, or report should never exceed eight lines.** Again, today's readers are intimidated by long chunks of information. They will read the first and last sentences and skim the middle. Therefore, to ensure your reader will not miss important information, keep paragraphs under eight lines long. Sample 1 shows a letter with long paragraphs; Sample 2 shows how the same text can be made more appealing and easier to read.

26. **Opening and closing paragraphs for email should be two to three lines long; body paragraphs should never exceed five lines.** Reading from a computer screen is more difficult than reading hard copy. If your email paragraph fills the screen, your reader may not try to interpret it. Make it easy on your reader — keep your paragraphs short.

APPEARANCE

27. **Appearance is important.** Most people don't plan the appearance of their documents. Yet how a letter, memo, email, or report looks plays a major role in whether or not the receiver reads it. If it appears too difficult to read, the receiver may ignore the material or put off reading it to a more convenient time.

SAMPLE 1
HARD-TO-READ LETTER

Dear Mr. Belmont:

As you are no doubt aware, personal computers play a paramount role in industry today. As these sophisticated systems take over more and more business functions, our dependence on them is growing dramatically. However, computers and peripheral equipment do break down. In fact, industry research indicates that the typical micro-computer system will need servicing at least twice a year. When it does, you are faced with downtime, reduced productivity, and often a large repair bill. The Echo Maintenance Agreement Program has been designed to combat the worries that often accompany extensive microcomputer usage, no matter how small or large your system may be.

Echo is qualified to service microcomputer and peripheral equipment for more than 40 manufacturers, including hundreds of product configurations. No matter what system your company has invested in, chances are that Echo can service it. Echo has been authorized by many manufacturers to provide full warranty service, thereby ending the delays in shipping your micro or peripheral equipment to a factory for repairs. In addition, we have set up nationwide service centers to provide you with a convenient, local service. Each center has an independent parts inventory as well as a link-up to our international inventory system.

You have the choice of pick-up delivery, carry-in, or on-site servicing — whatever is the most convenient and cost effective for you and your company's requirements.

... 2

EASIER-TO-READ LETTER

Dear Mr. Belmont:

Personal computers play a paramount role in industry today. As these sophisticated systems take over more and more business functions, our dependence on them is growing dramatically.

Computers and peripheral equipment, however, do break down. In fact, industry research indicates the typical microcomputer system will need servicing at least twice a year. When it does, you are faced with downtime, reduced productivity, and often a large repair bill.

What the Echo Maintenance Program Can Do for You

The Echo Maintenance Agreement Program has been designed to combat the worries often accompanying extensive microcomputer usage — no matter how small or large your system may be.

Echo is qualified to service microcomputer and peripheral equipment for more than 40 manufacturers, including hundreds of product configurations. No matter what system your company has invested in, chances are Echo can service it. Echo has been authorized by many manufacturers to provide full warranty service, thereby ending delays in shipping your micro or peripheral equipment to a factory for repairs.

Our Warranty Service

We have set up nationwide service centers to provide you with a convenient, local service. Each center has an independent parts inventory as well as a link-up to our international inventory system.

You have the choice of pick-up delivery, carry-in, or on-site servicing — whatever is the most convenient.

... 2

28. **White space is crucial.** White space is any space left unprinted. It includes the margins and the space between paragraphs and around lists. White space gives your readers' eyes a microsecond chance to rest and a microsecond chance to absorb the message. Documents with an attractive balance between white space and print appeal to readers. Although determining the correct balance is subjective, if you keep your paragraphs short, use lists, and use subheads, you will have an attractive, easy-to-read page.

29. **Margins are a key part of appearance.** All written documents should have margins at least one inch wide on all four sides. The margins will increase depending on the dictates of the letterhead and whether the document is bound.

    Letters should be centered between the top and bottom of the page; memos begin at the top of the page.

30. **Typefaces should be easy to read.** With today's word processors, you have access to numerous fonts. However, if you **use too many different ones**, you'll end up with a "ransom note" effect.

    Use only one serif (a typeface with short lines projecting from the strokes in each letter) and one or two **sans serif** (a typeface with no extra lines on the letters) typefaces per document. Text is generally easier to read in a serif typeface; for headings, overheads, slides, and computer screens it is better to use a sans serif typeface. Some serif fonts are Baskerville, Bookman, and Times Roman. Common sans serif fonts are Helvetica, Univers, and Avant Garde.

    A fairly common practice for reports is to use Times Roman or Garamond for the body and Helvetica or Arial for the headings and subheadings. You can vary the look by using different sizes of the two fonts; for example, use 18-point Helvetica for a heading and the same font at 14 points for a subhead. For a more complex report, you could use Univers for the headlines, Helvetica for the subheads, and Baskerville for the text. As a general guide, do not use more than three different fonts per document.

31. **Choose your font size carefully.** Don't choose a smaller font in an attempt to get all the information on one page. If your font size is so small and your margins so narrow that more than 90 characters fit on a line, your reader will have trouble reading the material. (When counting characters, include spaces and punctuation.)

    Likewise, your reader will find it difficult if you can fit only 30 characters on a line. This size of font causes rapid back-and-forth eye movement that is irritating.

    The size of font you choose depends on your typeface. If you are using Bookman, I suggest 12 point. Another common font and type size is 12-point Times Roman. However, if the message is lengthy, some people find this hard on the eyes.

    Before you decide on a particular font and type size, print out a few paragraphs in a variety of styles so you can choose the most readable one for your audience.

32. **Increase leading if type is small.** If your line contains more than 60 characters, add space between the lines to make the words easier to read. A good guideline is to set the line space — or leading (rhymes with "heading") — two points greater than the point size of the font.

    If you don't know how to increase the leading, ask your resident computer guru. It is a quick, simple step.

33. **Be careful when deciding whether to justify the type on your page.** Justification is the term given to how text is arranged on the page. If every line begins at the left margin and ends exactly at the right margin, the page is said to be justified. A nonjustified or, as it is sometimes called, a ragged right style is one where the lines end near, but not always exactly at, the right margin.

    Most people find text with a ragged right margin easier to read because of the even word spacing, logical word breaks, and additional white space.

34. **Never type the entire body of any document or email in capital letters, italics, or boldface.** Believing that it adds style or interest, some people use italics, boldface, or capitals for large portions of, or for the entire text of, a document. However, these typefaces are hard to read, and when they are overused they are not available for their usual function — to add special emphasis to a word or phrase.

    Never use italics for an entire business letter as they project an overly casual appearance.

    Note: One of the most common complaints about email is that senders often use all capital letters, making the message difficult to read.

35. **Use capital letters, boldface, and italics for emphasis only.** Use italics for emphasis, all capitals for more emphasis, and boldface to catch and hold the reader's eye. Don't get carried away. Don't underline the same information that you have already bolded. This is wasting a valuable tool. In addition, too much bolding or underlining distracts the reader from your message.

    Examples We can register you if you fill in the attached documents.

    FILL IN THE ATTACHED DOCUMENTS and we will register you.

    To be registered, **you must fill in the attached documents.**

    Wrong To be registered, **you must fill in the attached documents**. *(overkill)*

    Italics or underlining can be used for references to published works such as books, pamphlets, magazines, newspapers, and legislation.

    Examples Enclosed is a copy of our brochure *Holding a Successful Workshop*.

    Please note the article "Public Speaking for Shrinking Violets" in this month's *Successful Business* magazine.

36. **Subheads are ideal for breaking up long chunks of text.** Subheads appeal to readers. They make it easier to understand and interpret the message; they also make the writer look organized.

    In long letters, try to use at least one subhead per page — whenever you are making a new point. In reports, aim for a subhead every five or six paragraphs.

37. **Make your subheads as descriptive as possible.** The best subhead is one that adequately describes the upcoming information, so if readers only skim the material they will still have a basic understanding of your message. Subheads can run as long as seven or eight words.

    Example   Warranty Package

    Better   New Warranty Package for Large-Screen TVs

    Once you have written a letter, report, or other document, go over it with Checklist 1 and make sure your writing and presentation are as strong and clear as possible.

38. **The tone of your communications can win you friends or earn you enemies.** Tone is the way you express yourself in your communications with others. You can come across as boring, enthusiastic, caring, or overly formal. Tone is so important that Chapter 4 deals entirely with this topic. Read on.

CHECKLIST 1
BUSINESS WRITING STYLE

After you have written your document, ask yourself these questions:

WORD CHOICE

- ☐ Will my reader immediately understand each word?
- ☐ Did I use jargon, abbreviations, or acronyms? Were they appropriate and understandable?
- ☐ Did I use connecting words to move my reader through the message?

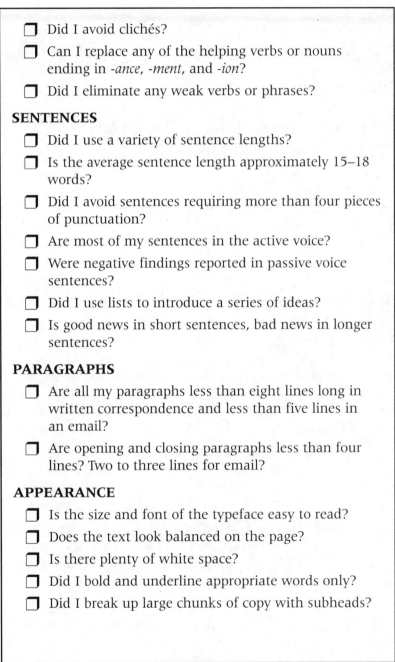

- ☐ Did I avoid clichés?
- ☐ Can I replace any of the helping verbs or nouns ending in *-ance*, *-ment*, and *-ion*?
- ☐ Did I eliminate any weak verbs or phrases?

SENTENCES

- ☐ Did I use a variety of sentence lengths?
- ☐ Is the average sentence length approximately 15–18 words?
- ☐ Did I avoid sentences requiring more than four pieces of punctuation?
- ☐ Are most of my sentences in the active voice?
- ☐ Were negative findings reported in passive voice sentences?
- ☐ Did I use lists to introduce a series of ideas?
- ☐ Is good news in short sentences, bad news in longer sentences?

PARAGRAPHS

- ☐ Are all my paragraphs less than eight lines long in written correspondence and less than five lines in an email?
- ☐ Are opening and closing paragraphs less than four lines? Two to three lines for email?

APPEARANCE

- ☐ Is the size and font of the typeface easy to read?
- ☐ Does the text look balanced on the page?
- ☐ Is there plenty of white space?
- ☐ Did I bold and underline appropriate words only?
- ☐ Did I break up large chunks of copy with subheads?

Chapter 4

26 WAYS TO ADD PERSONALITY TO YOUR WRITING AND WIN FRIENDS

In addition to clarity and conciseness, effective business correspondence must have an appropriate tone.

Tone is the way a message sounds. It adds personality to your writing. It turns messages into interesting and refreshing correspondence, or it reduces them to bland and boring documents. It can create goodwill and strengthen business relationships, or it can confuse and finally irritate readers. A poor tone makes a message — even an exciting one — uninteresting.

Example It is with our deepest and sincerest good wishes that we hereby wish to acknowledge receipt of the news that you have been appointed vice-president of your company.

Better Congratulations. We hear you are the new vice-president of Dohickeroo.

If you had to choose one of the following two writers to do business with, which one would you contact first?

Poor tone I would like to take this opportunity to thank you for visiting our booth at the COMTACTS show last week.

Enclosed are the brochures you requested.

If I can be of further assistance, please do not hesitate to contact me.

Yours truly,

Improved tone

I enjoyed talking with you at the COMTACTS show last week and discussing your plans for upgrading your system.

Enclosed are the brochures you requested. I believe the one titled *Computers and People: A necessary alliance* will answer many of your concerns regarding compatibility.

I will phone you next week after you have had a chance to go over the material. If you have any more questions, I'll be glad to answer them. If I can't, I'll put you in touch with our resident expert.

Regards,

Only one or two generations ago, it was the style for writers to produce letters and reports that all sounded alike. Anyone who refused to apply the established phrases and formats was considered eccentric or radical.

Now, especially in our letters and emails, readers want to see some personality. They want to know who they are doing business with. They want to feel a rapport between you and them, between your company and their company. Your tone is what does this for you. It involves sentence length and voice, word choice and contractions, and the way you address the reader. Tone can make you and your organization seem cold, unbending, and mechanical or pleasant, friendly, and caring.

DIFFERENT KINDS OF TONE

Here are four different ways to write the same message.

Cold	Please find enclosed documents regarding the widget project for your perusal. Your verbal analysis is required at the meeting scheduled for next Monday.
Formal	A report on the widget project is attached for your review. We would appreciate hearing your observations at next Monday's meeting.
Semi-formal	Please review the attached widget report. We look forward to hearing your comments at next Monday's meeting.
Informal	Here is the widget report. Please let us know what you think at Monday's meeting.

Notice that I haven't labeled these statements good, better, or best. Each statement (except for the one marked "Cold") is acceptable at different times. The tone must change according to the occasion (see Table 4). For example, if you are writing upward, that is, writing to people who are above you in the office hierarchy, you should adopt a semiformal tone rather than an informal one.

TABLE 4
TONE

FORMAL	SEMIFORMAL	INFORMAL
Annual reports	Letters	Letters (*to long-time associates*)
Technical reports	Memos, Reports	Memos
Formal minutes	Writing upward	Email messages

Normally, reports are written in a formal, impersonal tone. There are two reasons for this. First, there are usually several readers and the writer may not be familiar with each person. Second, good reports contain facts, statistics, and technical information. There is no room for the writer's personality and subjective viewpoint. Occasionally a report may be written in a less formal style, but this occurs only when the report is for in-house use and is going to a small, selected audience. This kind of report is usually written as a memo.

How do you write in a formal tone?

- Write all words in full. Don't use contractions such as *it's, can't,* and *don't* (replace them with *it is, cannot,* and *do not*).

- Refer to people by title or job description if necessary, not by their names.

- Avoid the words *I* or *me*, although a faceless *we* may be appropriate.

- Use passive verbs, particularly when presenting negative findings.

- Use longer sentences and paragraphs (but none over eight lines long).

Letters, memos, and emails are different. There is no reason they have to be dry and colorless. In fact, the majority should read as if a warm-blooded, live person wrote them.

Too many people believe they have to "change hats" when they write. And the hats they put on are heavy, unbecoming, and old-fashioned. These writers haven't stopped to realize what they are doing. They learned to write from their teachers and parents who in turn learned to write from their teachers and parents. Each generation carried on the language and tone of people and businesses no longer in existence.

This is illogical for today's business world, where people like things that are different. Now the most successful business correspondence possess a person-to-person, friendly air.

If you are uncertain how personable your correspondence sounds to others, read some of your letters and memos aloud.

Ask yourself:

- Does this sound like me?

- Are these the words I would use on the phone or when talking to someone?

- If I were the reader, how would I feel? Would I wish to do business with this person?

Some people have a natural gift for putting themselves into their message. However, if you are not happy with the tone of your messages, or feel there is room for improvement, here are some tips that are sure to help.

STARTING TO WRITE

1. **Begin by thinking about the reader and your purpose in writing.** Look at your message from the other person's viewpoint. Choose words you think the reader prefers, and arrange them in ways he or she won't resent.

2. **Relax when you write.** The best letters flow from the heart. They are simple, natural, and get to the point.

   Approach the task not as "I have to write to her" but as "I am going to talk to her." Do not take this too literally; don't use slang or ignore the rules of grammar. Just write in a respectful, friendly way — the same way you would talk to educated friends.

3. **Watch the opening words of your correspondence.** If you want to jump-start your letters, be careful with the first few words of your opening. Unnecessary fillers create a cold tone that is hard to warm up.

Example	I wish to take this opportunity to thank you for talking to me on the phone last week about job opportunities with your firm.
Better	Thank you for talking with me on the phone last week regarding job opportunities.

4. **Opening lines improve when you start with people rather than things.**

Example	Enclosed please find the brochure you requested.
Better	As you requested, here is the brochure.

5. **Don't start with a mention of office procedures.** Opening with words such as *according to our files* or *our records indicate* kills the reader's enthusiasm immediately. It gives people the impression you thought about them only when you were reminded to do so by your files.

Example	According to our files, you weren't happy with your latest shipment.
Better	I understand there were some difficulties associated with your latest shipment.

BEING COURTEOUS

6. **Use *I* more than *we*.** *We* means the organization and *I* means you personally. You can use both words in your correspondence. However, when it is practical and more accurate, use *I* over *we*. It adds personality to your writing and shows you are willing to take responsibility.

Example	If we can be of further assistance, please call us.
Better	If I can be of further assistance, please call me at (123) 555-4567.

7. **Use *you* more than *I* or *me*.** Everyone listens to radio station WIIFM (What's in it for me). You'll obtain a greater response from your readers when you spend more time talking to them than blowing your own horn.

Example	I am available at your convenience to discuss this issue further.
Better	If you wish to discuss this issue further, please let me know.

8. **Use personal words.** A good method for determining how appealing your message is to the reader is to count

the number of personal references. Personal references are words such as *I, me, you, he, she, it, we, they, your,* and *mine,* and names of people and companies. A rough guideline is that there should be six personal words for every 100 words.

Example   If the most recent business writing trends were tracked, it would be evident that an increased number of faxes and emails are being sent out to clients, customers, and staff. In addition, the number of formal business letters is most likely down from a few years ago. (*47 words, 0 personal references.*)

Better   If you were to track the most recent business writing trends, you would find an increased number of faxes and emails are being sent out to your clients, customers, and staff. The number of formal business letters you write is most likely down from a few years ago. (*48 words, 4 personal references.*)

9. **Use the reader's name.** A person's proudest possession is his or her name. Use it. When you are speaking, people can't tell if you are using the proper spelling, but they know in a letter. So check and double-check it.

   Use the name at least once in a one- to one-and-a-half-page letter, but don't tie it in with negative thoughts.

Example   I have not yet received your expense account, Jeff.

Better   Jeff, if you send me your expense account tomorrow, I can cut you a check before the weekend.

   If the salutation line begins formally with *Dear Mr. Jones,* stick with that name in the body of your letter. If it begins *Dear Greg,* use the first name in the body.

   To decide whether to call people by their first or last names, think about how you would address them if you were meeting them in their office. Remember, though, if you start with *Dear Suzanne*, you shouldn't switch back to *Dear Ms. Watson:* in future letters. It gives the impression you no longer wish to be friendly.

Note: If this is your first communication with a reader who is not part of your organization, don't use his or her first name. Many readers are irritated when someone they have never met becomes too friendly too fast.

10. **Avoid condescending words.** If you use words and phrases such as *obviously, it is clear,* and *as you are aware*, you may appear patronizing and could antagonize your reader.

Example Obviously, you are unaware of our refund policy.

Better Our refund policy covers ...

11. **Be polite.** When you ask someone to do something, it's common courtesy to add the words *please, thank you,* or *I would appreciate.* (Incidentally, the word *kindly* is old-fashioned and should not be used in business. Replace it with *please.*)

Examples Please call me next week with the details.

I'd appreciate a call next week regarding the details.

But make sure the words of courtesy fit. For example, don't start every letter with *thank you* or you'll sound insincere, particularly when you are responding to a letter of complaint.

Example Thank you for your letter of May 16 in which you complained about our service program.

Better After receiving your letter of May 16, I reviewed your concerns with our service department.

You can also use *thank you* to close your letter, if you haven't previously written it in the opening lines or body. The phrase *thank you again* smacks of insincerity or boredom.

12. **Smooth over awkward refusals with kind words.** Use conditional words such as *could, would, might, wish,* and *if* to soften refusals.

    Example   I cannot attend the strategic planning retreat.

    Better   I would attend the strategic planning retreat, but then I would miss my son's graduation.

    Example   I can't accept your invitation.

    Better   I wish I could accept your invitation.

13. **The more contractions you use, the more conversational your writing will sound.** *Don't, can't, won't,* and other contractions should be avoided in reports, but they work well when you want to adopt a less formal tone.

    Formal   The committee has not yet reached a decision.

    Semiformal The committee hasn't reached a decision yet.

    Informal   The committee hasn't decided yet.

SELLING YOUR MESSAGE

14. **Accentuate the positive.** Tell readers what you can do — not what you can't.

    Example   We cannot begin shipping until September 2.

    Better   We will begin shipping on September 2.

15. **Use short, informal sentences.** Incorporating shorter sentences gives you a more conversational tone.

    Example   I want to thank you for your consideration in telephoning me about your recent confusion over the policy.

    Better   Thank you for telephoning me about the policy.

16. **Turn a demand into a question, or use a cause-and-effect approach.** Instead of demanding readers do something immediately, soften your approach by phrasing the request as a question, or by telling them what you will do if they complete the task.

Example	You must sign this form and return it to us by February 15, or your name will not be added to the list of people who require snow shoveling.
Better	Will you please sign and return this form by February 15? That way we can add your name to the list of people who require snow shoveling. (*Question approach*)
Better	As soon as we receive the signed form, we will add your name to the list of people requiring snow shoveling. (*Cause-and-effect approach*)

17. **Use active voice rather than passive.** The active voice indicates you are taking responsibility for what is happening and reveals you as an individual.

Example	Your letter was received by us on May 2.
Better	I received your letter on May 2.

18. **Add a personal touch.** If you are writing to someone you know well, develop a personal touch. How can you do this? Include an extra line about that person, the city he or she lives in, a previous contact, or anything that may be of mutual interest. Usually "extras" are typed near the end of a letter, or written in ink when the writer signs it.

Example	I heard you were vacationing in Jamaica last week. I look forward to hearing your comments on that interesting island.

19. **Always explain benefits to your readers.** Too many writers, when listing features of a product or service, don't explain what benefit the reader will receive, leaving it up to the readers to work this out for themselves. When you are selling your readers on an idea, product, or service, spell out the advantages to them. Not only does this technique have a better audience response, but it also makes you appear more interested in, and knowledgeable about, your readers' needs.

Example	We have a 24-hour hotline service.
Better	Our 24-hour hotline guarantees you will never have to wait more than a few minutes for the answers to any of your questions.

20. **Put "sell" into everything you write.** Whenever you write, do something to stimulate goodwill. Even if you are just answering a simple request, remember the people who requested the information may spend money with your organization in the future. Is there anything you can write to confirm their judgment that they are dealing with a professional, caring person who works for an organization dedicated to its products and customer service? One extra sentence is sometimes all it takes to turn a routine reply into a positive selling tool.

Example	Here is the brochure you requested at the computer show.
Better	Here is the brochure you requested at the computer show. I have highlighted the paragraphs dealing with your specific software applications.

Example	Thank you for your interest in *Straight Talk*. The cost for 250 copies is 30¢ each. It would be a pleasure to serve you.
Better	Thank you for your interest in *Straight Talk*. We believe it is the best newsletter on business writing today. A number of companies use it to ensure their staff keep up to date with grammar rules and changes in writing styles. The cost for 250 copies is $75. As soon as we receive your check or purchase order, we'll send your order by courier.

21. **Pull, don't push, your readers.** Your readers will respond better if you try to interest them in doing what you want, rather than demanding they do it.

Example	Failure to provide us with your check by August 1 will mean a cancellation of your registration.
Better	If we do not receive your check by August 1, we will have to cancel your registration.
Better	If you send us your check by August 1, we will renew your registration.

22. **Send out brief congratulatory or thank-you notes.** One good way to keep your name in front of your customers and clients is to send out short notes congratulating them or thanking them for some activity. Yes, you could phone them, but chances are you'll end up on their voice mail. Besides, written statements produce a visual impact that remains longer in the memory. They can also be filed or shown to superiors and colleagues.

Take care, however, that these notes don't become routine. Each one should be a personalized message to the reader. When notes read as if they are prepared by someone else and barely glanced at by the person who signed them, they lose their value.

I recently met a real estate agent who told me she sends out eight thank-you messages a day. "Eight!" I exclaimed. It seemed like a lot. "Yes," she replied. "That's all I need in order to earn $250,000 a year." If she couldn't think of eight people to write to, she would go out and deliberately look for people and things she could praise.

23. **Be careful with humor. It may get you into trouble.** Humor is always good to relieve tension and get a point across in a lighter vein. However, people understand humor not only through words but also through body language and voice inflection. In letters, emails, and reports, readers do not have access to these clues and comments may be badly misinterpreted.

The membership chair of a large group once sent out the following statement: "I would personally appreciate your sending in your check because I have other things I would rather spend my limited time doing than following up with your renewal." The chair claimed it was written with tongue in cheek, but no one was amused. In fact, many members were irritated. How would you react?

In emails, many people use "smileys": symbols that replace body language. These are no longer considered professional in business messages.

24. **Never write when you are cross or irritable.** If you are annoyed, it will show up in your writing. No matter how you phrase the words, the tone will be abrupt and the reader will sense the upset. It is better to delay the writing to another time, or write the letter and give it at least a day's simmering period before you revise and mail it out.

Example   Please provide us with a letter outlining your specific requirements in terms of documentation from a builder in this situation so that we will no longer provide builders with an inconsistent message when we are advising them on the paperwork they must complete. (*The writer who penned these words was obviously ticked off.*)

Better   To ensure builders receive a consistent message on how to deal with this situation, please send us a memo stating the documents you require.

25. **Don't go overboard.** A pleasant, friendly tone is important, but don't overdo it, especially if you don't know the reader or if you know the reader prefers a more formal form of speech. And don't gush. It only makes you seem insincere.

Example   In spending so much time answering my questions last week, you rose even higher in my estimation and consolidated the fact that you are truly among the great individuals in life, dedicated to excellence and committed to assisting others in achieving their goals.

Better   I appreciate the time you took in answering my questions last week. I can see why so many people hold you in such high regard.

26. **Read your letters aloud.** Read your letter out loud and listen to it. Does it have a natural, friendly flow or is it choppy and demanding? If you were the reader, would you like the writer?

Your tone should be part of your overall business strategy. It is an expression of the business relationship you wish to foster with the reader. Initially, the tone should be semiformal, moving slowly toward the informal side as the business relationship and friendship develop. Be careful not to edge over to the informal too quickly, as it is hard to return to the formal relationship once you've gotten close.

Finally, when you have decided on the tone you wish to adopt, use it consistently throughout the entire letter. If you are writing to a dignitary, start with a formal tone and stay with it, even to the complimentary closing. If you begin with a conversational tone, don't become cold and impersonal halfway through. Always be consistent.

To make sure you maintain a consistent tone, evaluate your writing using Checklist 2.

CHECKLIST 2
APPROPRIATE TONE

After you have written your first draft, ask yourself:

☐ Did I think about the reader before I started the document?

☐ Did I deliberately choose a tone that reflects my relationship to the reader?

☐ Do the words sound natural and not stuffy?

☐ Do my opening words get quickly into the message and avoid boring the reader?

☐ Did I use more *you* words than *I* words?

☐ If I listed the features of any idea, service, or product, did I also include the benefits to the reader?

☐ Did I try to soften negative news?

☐ Is my tone consistent throughout the entire document?

☐ If I were the reader, would I like to do business with the writer of this document?

Chapter 5

42 WAYS TO MASTER LETTERS AND MAKE YOURSELF LOOK PROFESSIONAL ON PAPER

Emails are currently used more often in business than are letters. After all, emails are faster to send, require less work, and are more informal. However, I find that readers now have greater respect for letters than they used to. They realize the time and effort required to produce them, and they enjoy the "weight" of a document sent on letterhead or with a cover. Therefore, don't dismiss the importance of letters.

Each one is an opportunity to win friends, influence people, build better customer relations, and keep your name in front of existing or potential clients.

Letters can be sent to confirm or request information, deal with misunderstandings and complaints, sell new ideas and services, congratulate clients, and remind readers of your existence and expertise. The one thing to remember is that there is no such thing as a routine letter. As soon as an organization starts to regard external correspondence as a routine task, it loses its competitive edge.

For the purposes of this chapter, I have divided letter writing into three areas: organization, writing, and format.

ORGANIZATION

1. Before you start to write, think about how your readers will react to the contents of your letter. How will they feel about the message? Will they be happy, indifferent, or upset? This information will affect how you organize your correspondence. Use Worksheet 2 to plan your writing.

WORKSHEET 2
PLANNING TOOL FOR LETTERS

Reader's name

_____

What do you know about the reader? *(his or her background)*

_____

_____

How many times have you already discussed this topic with the reader?

☐ *Never*   ☐ *Once*   ☐ *More than once*

What does the reader want to know?

_____

_____

What do you want the reader to know?

_____

_____

What will the reader's reaction be to these points?

☐ *Good news*   ☐ *Mildly interested*
☐ *Indifferent*   ☐ *Bad news*

Based on the reader's reaction, what type of letter will you send?

☐ *Information*   ☐ *Bad news*   ☐ *Persuasion*

What do you want the reader to do after he or she is finished reading?

_____

_____

2. Routine business letters fall into one of three categories: information, bad news, and persuasion. Each one of these categories has a specific organizational pattern to help you deliver your message. The formats are outlined in Table 5. Examples of each kind of letter are shown in Sample 6 on page 62 and Samples 7 to 15 at the end of the chapter (starting on page 70).

3. If you are requesting or sending facts, use the information format. It is also called the direct approach because your reason for writing is in the first paragraph.

This format should be used when you are relaying good news. Remember to jump right in with the good news in the first paragraph. The reader will then pay close attention to the details. The information format is shown in Sample 3.

TABLE 5
FORMATS FOR WRITING LETTERS

TYPE OF LETTER		
Information	**Bad News**	**Persuasion**
Main idea/ Good news	Neutral idea	Attention-getter
Details	Background information	Introduce the idea, product, or service
	Bad news	Present details
		Benefits to the reader
Call for action	Neutral close	Call for action

SAMPLE 3
FORMAT FOR INFORMATION LETTER

	Dear Mark,
Main idea	Thank you for the information you provided for our home marketing campaign questionnaire. As always, your cooperation has helped ensure the success of this project.
Calling attention to details	I have enclosed a copy of the findings. Please note that some of this information is extremely sensitive and should be treated as confidential. These sections are marked.
Call for action	We'll be back to request an update in January. Again, Mark, thank you for your continued participation.
	Yours sincerely,

4. If your reason for writing is to convey unsettling news to the reader, use the bad-news format (see Sample 4). This uses the indirect approach, which means the receiver must read the background information before he or she learns your reason for writing — the bad news. Your reader may then be more receptive to the information. If readers are given the bad news first, they might skip the rationale or read it with a biased viewpoint.

Remember, it doesn't matter how *you* perceive the message; the important consideration is how your reader will react.

SAMPLE 4
FORMAT FOR BAD-NEWS LETTER

Dear Mr. Brown:

Neutral opening

In response to your letter of May 3, I contacted our national parts headquarters to locate the necessary part for your KV-18943 television.

Presenting facts

It is ABC's policy to always maintain a large stock of repair components for all our products. However, as we produce a wide range of goods, we have had to limit our inventory. We stock parts for a period of ten years after the last manufacturing date of a unit.

Supporting evidence

Bad news

Your model is over ten years old. We checked with our warehouse in Calgary and, as they did not have the part, asked them to contact their US and Japanese counterparts. We regret we were not successful in locating the required part.

Neutral ending

We trust you enjoyed your last ABC television, and it served you well, Mr. Brown. When the time comes to invest in another television, I recommend you visit your nearest ABC store at the North Common Shopping Center on Highway 7. I am sure you will be impressed by the knowledge and helpfulness of the salespeople and the wide range of our products.

Sincerely,

5. The persuasion format is used when you are selling your readers on a product, service, or idea. If you are writing a sales letter, you have only ten seconds to grab your reader's attention. If you don't get it in that time, your reader likely won't finish the letter.

   Research shows that sales letters of approximately one-and-a-half pages have the best reader response. Half-page letters and those over two pages have a lower response rate. Sample 5 is an example of the persuasion format.

6. Keep your letters short. Tell the reader only what he or she wants and needs to know. Be specific. Use a variety of sentence lengths — the average should be 18 words.

WRITING

7. Watch your opening sentence. Be specific; come to the point. For examples of lively opening lines, see Table 6.

   Example   We wish to acknowledge receipt of your letter of May 3. (*boring cliché*)

   Better   I have reviewed the concerns discussed in your letter of May 3.

8. Make each letter an individual talk. Be natural. Use words the reader can easily understand.

9. Emphasize the "you" attitude. Play the reader up, yourself down. Look at the problem from his or her point of view. Try to use *you* early in the sentence rather than *I* or *we*.

10. Whenever possible, avoid using negative words such as *inconvenienced, confused,* or *upset*. This only reminds readers of their earlier states, and they may be beyond this now.

    Example   We're sorry for any inconvenience that our product may have caused you.

    Better   Thank you for letting us know about this situation.

11. Reread the rules for tone in Chapter 4.

SAMPLE 5
FORMAT FOR PERSUASION LETTER

Begin with a point that the reader can agree with

Introduce the idea

Present request

Details and benefits

Call for action

Dear Ms. Smith:

ABC has always generously supported the Rainbow Ridge General Hospital. Your donation last year of $1,000 was a significant contribution to our 20-- campaign.

In this time of economic restraint, there is a large gap between available funds and the health care needs of the people of Rainbow Ridge. I am aware that ABC, like several other companies in the community, bases its corporate gift to the hospital on a per employee amount. However, we are asking you to rise to the current challenge and increase your donation from last year's $11.17 to $12.94 per employee for 20--.

The new amount represents the average per employee gift our top ten Rainbow Ridge companies donate, and it will make a difference to the health of our community members. In addition, your increased contribution will encourage other companies in the area to enlarge their donations.

I will call you next week to discuss ABC's contribution to the 20-- campaign.

On behalf of the staff of the hospital, who are dedicated to helping the residents of Rainbow Ridge, I would like to send thanks, Ms. Smith, to both you and ABC.

Yours sincerely,

TABLE 6
OPENING LINES

The following opening lines should be used only to jump-start your own creative processes. Think about why you are writing and then come up with your own original opening.

We were pleased to receive your order for 23 lamp shades.

Thank you for sending us one of your motivational lithographs.

Here's the information I promised you last month.

Congratulations! I hear you have just been made king.

I've enclosed the Kingsley Report. It should answer your questions.

I enjoyed meeting you at the COMMIXED exhibit and discussing your future computer plans.

Thank you for talking with me last week regarding your training needs.

Your remarks regarding our new financial package made me revisit the proposal.

The books you ordered are being shipped today.

Ms. Gloria Dezell suggested I call you regarding ...

I'm sorry to hear you are not happy with the conciliation arrangements.

I've read the suggestions in your letter and will review them with my staff.

It's that time again. Our membership year starts April 1.

You've already seen the dramatic difference our professional lawn care can make.

We wish to add our names to the list of those people opposed to ...

Welcome to our banking family!

Are you paying too much for ... ? There are ways to reduce it.

We appreciate your taking the time to inquire about ...

TABLE 6 — **Continued**

On behalf of the … , I would like to congratulate the Credit Valley Hospital for receiving a four-year accreditation.

Thank you for visiting my dealership and allowing my staff to assist you.

You're right. We did make an error.

Thank you for allowing me to introduce you to the many, varied services of ABC productions.

Please make the following adjustments to my account.

Informal openings when omitting a salutation line:

Yes,
  Mr. Smith,
        the posters you require are available for immediate shipping.

You are right, Mr. Thomas,
        poor service is not tolerated at Upstairs Downstairs.

We're delighted, Ms. Garrett,
        that you have chosen us to host your Gala Ball.

I need your help, Susan, to meet our year-end deadline.

12. In an information or good-news letter, call the reader by name at least once in a one- to two-page letter. Make sure you spell his or her name correctly.

13. Develop your letter step by step. Make it logical. Use connecting words and subheads. Keep paragraphs less than eight lines long.

14. Specify definite dates and actions. Don't be vague.

15. Avoid clichés. Refer to Table 3 in Chapter 3 for alternatives to common clichés.

16. Always close with a call for action. Let your readers know what you want them to do next — call you, write to you, or wait for you to call them. Sometimes you may not want any action except to understand the information, file it, or think of you in a favorable light. But whatever you want, let the readers know. Table 7 lists closing lines you might use.

Example If you have any questions, please don't hesitate to contact me. (boring cliché)

Better If you have any questions, please call me at (123) 555-7890.

FORMAT

17. Letters begin with the date and follow with the name and address of the reader. This information is normally typed in upper- and lowercase; however, some organizations prefer to use only capital letters for the inside address so that it matches the envelope requirements of the postal service (see the examples at Rule 42).

18. If you are sending a letter by fax or by email and then sending the original by mail, make a reference to this fact so that readers will not be confused when they receive the second copy. Type *Sent by fax* or *Via email* at the left margin under the inside address, or align it with the right margin.

Example

March 1, 20--

Ms. Helen Smith
Conference Coordinator
Humber College
205 Humber College Boulevard
Etobicoke ON M9W 5L7

Via fax *(If you are not mailing the original, delete this reference line.)*

TABLE 7
CLOSING LINES

I will call you next week after you have had a chance to read the material.

I will call you within the next few days to arrange a convenient time to meet.

I look forward to meeting with you on June 3.

As soon as I receive your check, I will proceed with your registration.

To take advantage of this offer, you must respond by January 30.

We look forward to working with you.

I will call you in mid-March to see how you are progressing.

To complete the report, I need the information by May 30.

All of us at ... wish you the very best of the season.

If you would like more information, please let me know. My number is ...

Fill in and return the enclosed card, Ms. Smith, and your registration at the conference will be assured.

Looking forward to hearing of your progress.

I will call you next week to further discuss putting my expertise to work for (company name).

We appreciate the job you are doing for us.

It's a pleasure to have the opportunity to assist you.

I'm sorry we can't be more helpful.

If you haven't sent us your check already, will you please mail it today?

Your reports are usually prompt — what happened this time? We need it immediately.

The check will be in the mail early next month.

Thank you for your patience.

If you need more information, just write to ...

If you are sending a one-page letter to a small organization or to someone who sits near a fax machine, you can get away without using a cover sheet. Otherwise, use a fax cover sheet.

19. A reference line containing a file, policy, invoice, or order number may be included for file purposes. This information always appears one to two lines under the date.

Example | March 1, 20--
|
| Reference #17540 - 620499
|
| Ms. Helen Smith
| Conference Coordinator
| Humber College
| 205 Humber College Boulevard
| Etobicoke ON M9W 5L7

20. It is common business practice to use the reader's title of *Mr.* or *Ms.* in the inside address and the salutation line. (If a woman prefers to be referred to as *Miss* or *Mrs.*, she should sign her letters with this title — see Rule 34. It is then the reader's responsibility to ensure that all future correspondence is addressed correctly.) Doctors are addressed as Dr. Brown or as Susan Brown, MD. Do not mix these two styles.

Examples   Dear* Mr. Green:

Dear Ms. Blakey:

Dear Dr. Brown:

---

*Some writers don't want to use *Dear* because they feel the reader is not their *dear*. However, this salutation is traditional and many readers would be upset if it were missing from a letter. I have listed a few options in Table 6 that writers might use as informal openings in direct mail, promotional material, and customer service letters. You have to be careful when and where you use them, but I think we will see a lot more of these informal openings in the future.

21. Many writers are dropping the *Mr.* and *Ms.* from the inside
     address and the salutation line. This works well when you
     do not know the sex of the reader and do not have time to
     find out. The same tactic applies if you are unsure of which
     name is the surname. In these instances, use the reader's
     full name.

Examples   Dear Chris Stone:

Dear R.J. Deakin:

Dear Young Kil:

22. If you do not have a name, address the letter to the position.

Example | March 1, 20--
|
| Human Resources Manager
| Onsite and Customized Programs Division
| Canadian Management Centre
| 5th Floor, 150 York Street
| Toronto ON M5H 3S5
|
| Dear Human Resources Manager:

23. If you do not have a name or position, omit the salutation
     line and use a subject line only. Subject lines start at the
     left margin or are centered on the page. See Sample 6 for
     an example of this type of letter.

Example | March 1, 20--
|
| Onsite and Customized Programs Division
| Canadian Management Centre
| 5th Floor, 150 York Street
| Toronto ON M5H 3S5
|
| Request for Information

September 15, 20--

<u>Recommendation for Timothy Russell</u>

This letter is to recommend Timothy Russell as an out-standing salesperson.

I've known and worked with Tim for more than three years. He is a highly responsible and creative individual. From the day he came to work for us, he was a welcome member of our sales team. He willingly undertook any task assigned him, whether it involved direct sales or not, and his enthusiastic and infectious manner made him popular with all our customers.

I am sorry to lose Tim, but his educational plans call for him to move outside our city. I believe anyone who hires him will be truly fortunate.

Sincerely,

John Watson
Owner

gac

24. Attention lines, and the terms *To Whom It May Concern, Dear Sir/Madam,* or *Ladies and Gentlemen,* are considered old-fashioned and should not be used.

25. Use a colon with a formal salutation: *Dear Ms. Smith:* Use a comma with an informal salutation: *Dear Robert,*

26. Some writers use a formal salutation line with *Mr.* or *Ms.* Then, when they are signing the letter, they slash through the name and write the receiver's first name by hand. They believe it gives their letters a personal touch. This technique works with form letters, but is not recommended for normal correspondence. It gives the impression the sender only thought about who the reader was after the letter was written.

27. The subject line is optional when using a salutation. It usually appears below the salutation and above the first line of the message. The subject line may be introduced by the word *Subject* or some variation of it, or the word may be omitted. The subject line can be placed at the left margin, or centered for emphasis.

Example | March 1, 20--

Ms. Helen Smith
Conference Coordinator
Business & Industrial Services
Humber College
205 Humber College Boulevard
Etobicoke ON   M9W 5L7

Dear Ms. Smith:

Subject: Request for information

Examples *(subject line variations)*

SUBJECT: FIRST YEAR WARRANTY
              PROTECTION

Re: Employment status of William Colgate

Refer to Policy 657-678

Request for information

28. You may use *I* and *we* in the same letter. *I* means you as an individual. *We* means your whole organization.

29. Remember that opening and closing paragraphs should not exceed four lines. The paragraphs of the body should not exceed eight lines.

30. Make your letter look attractive. Use equal margins with lots of white space.

31. The acceptable closings for today's letters are *Sincerely, Yours sincerely,* or *Regards. Regards* is used when writing to a business associate who is also a personal friend.

    Yours truly is used nowadays for more formal writing, such as when writing to people in ecclesiastical or diplomatic circles.

32. If you are sending a one-page letter on company stationery, it is redundant to include the company name under the complimentary closing. If your letter flows on to a second page without a logo, however, you can add the company name in capitals.

Example | *(nonletterhead paper)*

Sincerely,

FIRTH WIDGET COMPANY

Greg Firth
Greg Firth
President

33. The writer's name and title are normally typed four lines below the complimentary closing or the company name. If the letter is short you could leave six lines; if it is long, reduce the space to two lines.

34. Usually a man does not type *Mr.* in his signature, but if he has a name that could be mistaken for a woman's and he wants to ensure that the reader knows who he is, he should use *Mr.* in either his handwritten signature or his typed signature. The same advice holds true for women who want to be referred to as *Mrs.* or *Miss.*

Example	Regards,	Sincerely,
	Kris Burton	*Mr. Kris Burton*
	Mr. Kris Burton	Kris Burton
	Executive Assistant	Executive Assistant

35. If a secretary is asked to sign a letter on behalf of the boss, it is now customary for the secretary to sign the boss's name and add his or her initials. An alternative is for the secretary to sign the letter in his or her own name.

Example	Sincerely,	Yours sincerely,
	Julia Taush (m.g.)	*Michelle Gutkin*
	Ms. Julia Taush	Michelle Gutkin
	Marketing Director	Secretary to Ms. Taush

36. The typist's initials may be placed at the left margin in upper or lower case. Adding the writer's initials is redundant because the writer's name is already in the signature block. The practice of adding initials is fading as many people now type their own material.

37. If you are including one or more items with your letter, type the word *Enclosure* — or some variation — at the left margin, two lines under the typist's initials, or under the signature block if there is no need for the typist's initials.

Example	Sincerely,
	Julia Taush
	Ms. Julia Taush
	Marketing Director
	Enclosure

Examples *(enclosure line variations)*

Enclosure *or* Enclosures
Encl. *or* 2 Encl. *or* Encl. (2)
Attachment *or* Attachments
Att. *or* 2 Att.

38. Use of the term *c.c.* to indicate other recipients of a letter is under debate. Some people use *c.c.* because it is traditional, and they are used to seeing it on their email messages. Others dislike it because it refers to carbon copies, and they aren't using carbons anymore. Alternatives are to use a single *c* or to spell it out when sending hard copy messages, *Copy to.*

No matter which alternative you use, the information is placed at the left margin, two lines below any preceding information.

Example	Sincerely,
	Julia Taush
	Ms. Julia Taush
	Marketing Director
	Copy to Paul Becevello *(There is no punctuation as it is on one line.)*
	Copy to: *(Note the use of a colon — a list follows.)*
	Sabrina Anzini
	Paul Becevello
	Greg Firth
	Linda Mackay-Watson

39. A postscript, or *PS*, works well with direct mail letters to emphasize a key selling point. However, avoid using a *PS* when preparing normal business correspondence. It can make you look disorganized.

Example *(for a direct mail piece)*

> PS: Remember this offer is valid only until September 30.

The postscript should be typed two to four lines below every other part of the letter, including the *Copy to* and *Enclosure* lines. Leave two spaces between the *PS* and the first word of the message. The margins should be the same as for the body of the letter.

40. Today most business letters are typed in one of three styles: block, modified block, or modified semi-block.*

In the block style, which is the most common, all parts are aligned with the left margin, including the date, inside address, subject line, text, signature block, and the continuation page heading. The right side is ragged. See Samples 7, 10, and 13.

The modified block style — shown in Samples 8, 11, and 14 — is similar, except the date is centered on the page or placed about five spaces to the left of the center. The complimentary close and the signature block are aligned under the date. The continuation page heading is spread across the top of the page.

Samples 9, 12, and 15 show the modified semi-block style. Here the first line of each paragraph is indented six spaces. The right side is ragged; the date, complimentary close, and signature block are centered, placed five spaces to the right of the center, or aligned with the right margin. The continuation page heading is spread across the top of the page.

---

*To ensure correspondence projects a professional, consistent look to clients and customers, everyone within an organization should use the same layout design. The chosen design should be explained in the company style book and distributed to all employees.

41. If the message continues on to a second page, use a blank second sheet of the same size, color, and texture as the letterhead page. The margins should match. On the top of the second page, type the continuation page heading. This contains the name of the recipient, page number, and date. Do not use abbreviations.

Example *(block style)*

Page 2
Ms. Linda Mackay-Watson
August 30, 20--
Reference Number 23-456-98 *(optional)*

Example *(modified and modified semi-block style)*

Ms. Linda Mackay-Watson - 2 - August 30, 20--
Reference Number 23-456-04 *(optional)*

Samples 9, 10, and 14 show two-page letters with continuation page headings in each of the styles.

42. On envelopes, the post office requests all addresses be typed flush left, and written or typed in all capitals with no punctuation marks unless they are part of a place name (e.g., ST. JOHN'S).

Examples   MR. COLIN THOMAS
ACCOUNT MANAGER
MICRO-MACROS INC
323 LAKESHORE ROAD
CRYSTAL CITY SK K5K 3B3
CANADA *(if required)*

MR. COLIN THOMAS
ACCOUNTANT MANAGER
MICRO-MACROS INC
323 LAKESHORE ROAD
CRYSTAL CITY MA 32119-4678
USA *(if required)*

In Canadian addresses, the two-letter province abbreviation is separated from the postal code by two spaces.

In American addresses, separate the zip code from the state abbreviation by two spaces. The zip code may be either five or nine digits. If the nine digit format is used, there will be a hyphen between the fifth and sixth digits.

Use the country name only if your letter is being sent outside your country.

Once you've written and typed your letter, evaluate it against the points on Checklist 3.

CHECKLIST 3
LETTERS

After you have composed a letter, ask yourself:

- ☐ Did I think about my reader before I began to write?
- ☐ Did I analyze the reader's reaction to the message and organize the letter appropriately?
- ☐ Did I tell my reader what he or she wants and needs to know? Is all other information eliminated?
- ☐ Does the set up of the letter meet my company's directives?
- ☐ Does the page look inviting to read?
- ☐ Is there plenty of white space and wide margins?
- ☐ If the letter is longer than one page, did I break up the copy with subheads?
- ☐ Will the opening line interest the reader?
- ☐ Are all the paragraphs under eight lines?
- ☐ Are opening and closing paragraphs no longer than four lines?
- ☐ Do any of the details in the body fit into lists? (See Sample 9.)
- ☐ Are there any clichés?
- ☐ Did I close with a call for action?

SAMPLE 7
INFORMATION LETTER
(Block style)

March 1, 20--

Reference number 01 09 123

Sent by fax — 2 pages

Ms. Helen Smith
Conference Coordinator
Business & Industrial Services
Humber College
205 Humber College Boulevard
Etobicoke ON M9W 5L7

Dear Helen,

Quote for printing brochure

This letter confirms our telephone conversation of February 27, regarding the printing of your publication, *Supervisory Summit*.

The cost of the printing will be $874.89. A specification sheet outlining the cost breakdown is attached.

I have enjoyed working with you on other publications, Helen, and know you will be happy with the quality of this one.

If you send me the rough copy by March 30, I can put it into the following Monday's production schedule so your publication will be ready by April 6. I will call you later this week to confirm the order.

Yours sincerely,

Peter Jansen
Peter Jansen

Printing Coordinator

Att.

SAMPLE 8
INFORMATION LETTER
(Modified block style)

March 22, 20--

M.A. SMITH
1243 SPEERS ROAD
NEW YORK NY 99888-1234

Dear M.A. Smith:

Enclosed is the information you requested on CLARITY's Extended Service Plans.

As I explained on the phone, the cost of purchasing our Gold Plan, which includes in-home service, would be $137.82 (taxes included).

I understand you purchased your television from Moonlight TV and Audio on April 17, 20--. Please confirm this purchase by filling in the attached form and returning it to me. Remember to detach the claim form from the registration card, as you will need it for future service.

I look forward to receiving the registration card and your check or money order so I can add your name to our register of satisfied Gold Plan customers.

Sincerely,

Gail Seymour
Gail Seymour

Account Representative

Encl.

SAMPLE 9
INFORMATION LETTER WITH A LIST
(Modified semi-block style)

September 1, 20--

Ms. Joanne Dearborn
ABC International Trainers
123 Florence Lake Road
Victoria BC V8V 1A2
Canada

Dear Joanne,

Thank you for your interest in *MJW* Communications. As requested, I am enclosing the information you require for the Asian assignment.

MJW Communications is a business consulting firm that offers workshops and individual consultations to corporations. Our topics include:

- presentation skills
- business writing
- listening skills
- voice projection
- meeting management
- international protocol

Our programs are conducted by a team of facilitators known for their expertise in their particular fields, as well as for the high caliber of their delivery skills. In addition, because our high-content sessions are interactive and highly customized, workshop participants leave the sessions with useful information that can be implemented immediately. Naturally, we offer a money-back satisfaction guarantee.

Page 2   Ms. Joanne Dearborn   September 1, 20--

Joanne, I am confident *MJW* Communications can meet your needs. I will call you within the week, after you have had a chance to read the attached information. If you wish to reach me in the meantime, please call me at (905) 555-9909.

Sincerely,

Jane Walters

Jane Walters

Principal

Encl.

SAMPLE 10
BAD-NEWS LETTER
(Block style)

September 3, 20--

Reference number 034-8961

Mr. Joseph E. Smithers
President, ABC Distributors
18th Floor
125 48th Avenue E.
Seattle WA 12345

Dear Mr. Smithers:

In January of 20--, ABC Distributors signed an agreement
with Rainbow to become the sole distributor of Rainbow's
XXX product line across the United States.

Both companies were pleased with the initial growth pattern
and new sales targets were enthusiastically agreed upon by
both parties.

Since December of 20--, however, there has been a dramatic
decline in the sale of our products through your company. By
the end of July, your sales were only $423,000 or 40 percent of
the goals set for the first half of this fiscal year. And you have
not given us any indication there is hope for improvement
over the next few months.

Obviously, part of this can be attributed to the depressed
market. However, our major concern is that since the time
ABC reorganized its management staff, there has not been
a national distribution plan for the sale of our products.

We still believe a national distributor is the most effective
method for Rainbow to build its customer base, and we
hope our product line complements your product mix in the
business machine marketplace. However, we must establish

Page 2
Mr. J.E. Smithers
September 3, 20--
Reference number 034-8961

Rainbow's position in the marketplace, and it is possible we may be forced to consider other distribution channels.

I would like to get together within the next two weeks, Mr. Smithers, so we can discuss specific plans for the future and establish exactly where Rainbow products fit into your company's planning.

I will call you at the end of the week to arrange a time and location.

Sincerely,

James N. Snow

James N. Snow

Vice President

jmb

Copy to Susan Blakey

SAMPLE 11
BAD-NEWS LETTER
(Modified block style)

May 1, 20--

Mr. Roy Nelson
Motivational Lithographs Inc.
124 Rogers Road
Crystal City ON L7H 7Y7

Dear Mr. Nelson:

Jean-Luc Boisvert has asked me to thank you for getting in touch with us regarding your company's motivational lithographs.

Because we strongly believe in creating specifically tailored communications for precisely defined audiences, we do not have a need for such lithographs, although they are truly breathtaking.

Thank you for thinking of us.

Sincerely,

Alexandra Lobach

Alexandra Lobach

Administrative Assistant

SAMPLE 12
BAD-NEWS LETTER
(Modified semi-block style)

February 6, 20--

Mr. S. Leacock
President
Thompson Shipping Inc.
45 Center Street
Austin TX 55577

Dear Mr. Leacock:

Galaxy International and Thompson Shipping Inc. have enjoyed a mutually profitable working relationship for two years now.

Our credit department has recently notified me that over the past three months, Thompson Shipping has billed us for handling charges on shipments to your warehouses.

Although there has never been an agreement between Thompson and Galaxy to pay handling charges, Thompson has deducted $614.78 from our monthly payments to cover this charge. Apparently the additional costs are for service charges and defective products. However, our records show there were no problems with these shipments.

I am sure this problem is an unfortunate oversight. Please return the $614.78 to Galaxy so we will not have to reduce your volume incentive rebate by that amount.

I look forward to receiving your check and to many more years of good relations.

Sincerely,

Marion Bradley

Marion Bradley

General Manager

Copy to Margaret Smith
Accounting Department

SAMPLE 13
PERSUASION LETTER
(Block style)

February 1, 20--

Mr. Donald Therrien
145 Islington Avenue, Unit 6
Fredericton NB E3A 1K9

Dear Mr. Therrien:

If a company is to continue to grow in today's marketplace, it must have great products, provide good service, and listen to its customers.

We at Krypton International pride ourselves on the quality and performance of our products and our customer service. However, we are interested in hearing your experience with Krypton. We know you purchased a camcorder from a Krypton store three months ago. Now that you have had time to use it, we would like to know how you feel about the machine. Would you recommend it to your friends? How do you feel about our sales staff? Were they knowledgeable and helpful?

The attached questionnaire asks 20 simple questions, all related to our products and service. It should take no more than ten minutes to complete. We have even included a pen — yours to keep — to help you get started.

By taking the time to fill in this survey, you will be helping us to assist you in the future with new and improved merchandise and service.

Please return the form to us in the attached, self-addressed envelope. Thank you for your cooperation.

Regards,

James Ross
James Ross

Customer Service

Encl (3)

SAMPLE 14
PERSUASION LETTER
(Modified block style)

April 9, 20--

Ms. Catherine Saito
President
Deluxe Apparel Inc.
1 Park Street
Crystal City MA 32119-4678

Dear Ms. Saito:

If we could cut your production time, increase your sales, and decrease your administrative costs would you be interested?

It is true. We can do this and much, much more through computerized information management — a necessity for growing apparel and textile operations.

Supreme, a "Fortune 400" super manufacturer, and Rogers & Jones, a leading developer of software for the sewn products industry, have joined forces to provide computer solutions for the apparel and textile markets.

Rogers & Jones is also recognized throughout the United States and Canada for TABS (Textile Apparel and Business Systems) Software.

The enclosed literature shows how ... (*one to two paragraphs on what you want the reader to particularly notice in the brochures*).

Ms. Catherine Saito   - 2 -   April 9, 20--

There are also other solutions we would like to discuss with you personally.

I will telephone you next week to arrange an appointment.

         Sincerely,

         ROGERS & JONES
         SOFTWARE

         Natalia Lobach
         Accounts Manager

3 Encl

SAMPLE 15
PERSUASION LETTER
(Modified semi-block style)

October 31, 20--

Ms. A. Tippler
Marketing Manager
ABC Realty
123 Ellerslie Avenue
Miami FL 33322

Dear Ms. Tippler:

It was a pleasure speaking with you today about our sub-scription service for Cobden Region, Financial Information Services (FIS).

FIS is a cost-effective monthly publication combining mortgage information with property transaction data. Each monthly edition is comprised of three sections: sales, mort-gage registrations, and mortgages coming due. The enclosed flier describes this breakdown in more detail.

The price for each monthly issue is just $150 (plus taxes). For an additional 20 percent you can also obtain the informa-tion on computer disks. If you are planning any mass mail-ings, the computerized information will simplify the task enormously.

Ms. A. Tippler   -2-   October 31, 20--

    FIS will help you increase your business by allowing you to reach hundreds of qualified mortgage prospects every month. Can you afford not to take advantage of this opportunity?

    I will call you in a few days, Ms. Tippler, to answer any questions you might have on FIS and on how it can expand your market base.

                             Regards,

                             Jessie Williams
                             Account Manager

Encl

Chapter 6

42 WAYS TO WRITE EMAILS THAT WILL INCREASE YOUR CHANCES OF GETTING READER BUY-IN

Emails have become an established part of the business world. In fact, some studies show that the average employee now spends six hours a week sending and receiving email messages.

However, I find that most people have a love/hate relationship with this tool. We enjoy emails because they permit us to communicate quickly and in our own timeframe. We can quickly send a message to a colleague or to a group of people whenever we wish, and can then cross the task off our "to do" list. They make us efficient.

They also give us a paper trail for reference, planning, and protection.

On the other hand, we receive too many emails and this impacts our effectiveness. It is time consuming to determine the importance of each message we receive, decide how to handle it (act on it, file it, or delete it), and prepare a response if necessary.

In addition, emails can affect our professional image. It is no longer acceptable to have sloppy, poorly written emails. Readers frequently complain about the tone of a message, spelling and grammatical errors, and rambling ideas. (For more information on tone, please read Chapter 3.)

Another problem with emails is that the tool is often used incorrectly. Often, phoning, writing, or meeting is a better way to communicate. How do you decide which one to use? There are five areas to consider:

- Speed
- Distribution
- Retrieval
- Impression
- Purpose

If you want to send a message quickly, emails are wonderful. If you want to obtain information quickly, it is often better to phone. When distributing the same information to a large group, emails excel. However, if you want your readers to be able to retrieve the information sometime in the distant future, you are better off sending the information in a hard copy version. (The average person tends to be able to retrieve hard copy documents more easily when they are physically filed.)

If you want to leave a strong, professional image in your reader's mind about yourself and your organization, send a hard copy document on letterhead or with a fancy cover. People tend to value what they can hold in their hands.

In addition, your purpose for writing should have a major impact on your choice of communications tool. If you want to negotiate or resolve an issue, do it face to face, or at least by phone. You need to see the body language and to hear the tone of voice. I also believe that if you have exchanged emails on a specific topic at least three times but have not moved ahead, you need to pick up the phone.

When choosing how to communicate, you should also consider the relationship you want to build. I have heard numerous complaints from people about receiving emails from coworkers who could easily have asked a question or delivered information face to face. Be careful not to hide behind your computer when conveying simple messages. Business people still enjoy meeting when it is convenient to do so.

FORMAT

All emails are equipped with *To, Cc,* and *Subject* lines.

1. Anyone whose name appears on the *To* line is expected to
    take action on the message. Anyone whose name is on the
    Cc line is being sent the information for interest only —
    unless the writer has indicated otherwise in the body of
    the message. However, I believe this is a dangerous prac-
    tice as people don't read messages as quickly or as care-
    fully when they are just being copied. If you want action,
    keep people's names on the *To* line.

2. The *Bcc.* line on an email is a wonderful tool — if used cor-
    rectly. If you send a message to a large group of people and
    anyone chooses to print it, his or her name as well as the
    names of everyone on the *To* and *Cc* lines will appear first
    on the page. Sometimes, depending on the number of re-
    ceivers, your message may not start until near the end of
    the printed page.

    If the receivers do not need to know the addresses of
    everyone who has received the message, then why not put
    the names on the *Bcc.* line? That way, if the message is
    printed, space is not wasted with useless information. Of
    course, you would identify the people who received the
    message in your salutation in the body of the message.

    Example   (*salutation line*)

    > To all members of the Executive Women's
    > Golf Association

3. Subject lines are crucial in an email. Some people even
    delete without reading any message that does not contain
    a subject line. Subject lines help people to decide whether
    to read a message and where to file it. That's why an email
    should only carry information related to one topic. We will
    discuss subject lines in more detail in the section "Surviv-
    ing a Reader's Inbox."

4. Emails are less formal documents than letters. They are
    often considered closer to a phone call or a meeting. If you
    were to meet someone for the first time that day, you

would probably start the conversation with *Hello, Hi, Good morning,* etc. Therefore, your first email of the day to a person should start with a similar greeting. If you are exchanging messages with the same person all day, you can drop the greeting as the day progresses.

In North America, emails should not start with *Dear.* (In some European and Asian countries, however, *Dear* is still being used. I recommend using the custom of the country you are writing to.)

Here are some suggestions for salutations depending on your relationship with the reader:

Formal	Casual	Personal
Hello	Hi	Reader's first name
Both names of reader	Everyone	
Greetings	Good day	

Personally, I do not like Good morning or Good afternoon. If the reader does not have an opportunity to read the message in the same time frame as you have written, it may come across as a "hand slap."

5. Because messages are harder to read from a computer screen, you need plenty of white space to make your document appear easier to read. Therefore, keep your paragraphs short — no longer than five lines and leave a blank line between paragraphs (see Sample 16).

   Sample 17 also shows how a message can be made clearer by using the connecting words we discussed in Chapter 3, and by using more informal words.

6. People want to read an email the same way they read a morning newspaper. Therefore, use appropriate punctuation and don't distract your reader from your message with unusual spacing.

7. Do not indent and do not prepare an email that consists of one-line sentences with double spacing between the paragraphs. This is visually distracting.

SAMPLE 16
POOR EMAIL

(This message lacks visual appeal, connecting words, a salutation, and a closing line. In addition, the wording is outdated.)

As per your email, our IT strategy for STARBRIGHT is to have a reduction in the number of vendors we deal with to simplify the paperwork. We want to increase the leverage we have with our primary suppliers. Astro and Fuller are our telecom providers for data networks. Astro already provides very good service for our data communications in the western region, and also on our participant network in Toronto. We use Fuller for telephone circuits only. IT believes that moving our cell phone business to Astro will improve our leverage with this vendor and simplify the paperwork. Remaining with Fuller will not provide us any strategic advantage.

SAMPLE 17
REVISED EMAIL

Harinder,

As you requested, our IT strategy is to reduce the number of vendors we deal with so we can simplify the paperwork. And we want to increase the influence we have with our primary suppliers.

Currently, Astro and Fuller are our telecom providers for data networks. Astro already provides very good service for our data communications in the western region and also for our participant network in Toronto. But we use Fuller for telephone circuits only.

Therefore, IT believes that remaining with Fuller will not provide us any strategic advantage. On the other hand, moving our cell phone business to Astro will give us more influence with this vendor and simplify the paperwork.

Regards,

The following email breaks the rules for good visual appeal.

Rose,

Thank you...........You are correct...........Balwinder Gangadeen is the successful candidate for the P/T position previously vacated by Rory Sheehan.........we will now need to find a casual replacement for Balwinder. The necessary document will be completed this evening and left to your attention.

Thanks.

---

8. Although many writers don't think it is important, poor spelling and grammar distracts your reader from your message. Turn on your electronic spell checker.

9. You can use abbreviations and acronyms in an email as long as the reader will understand them.

10. As emails can carry lengthy information (disclaimers) below your message, it is important to indicate that your message is coming to an end by inserting a complimentary close.

The following are examples of closing phrases for different styles of emails:

Formal	Casual	Personal*
Regards	Thanks	Cheers
Thank you		Bye
		Happy Holidays
		TGIF
		Ciao

11. Every email should carry a signature box. The signature box tells the reader all the ways you are willing to be contacted. Ideally, signatures should not be longer than five lines. I recommend people have two signature boxes — one for external communication, the other for internal.

---

* Any abbreviation or personal close the reader will understand.

A signature box on an external message should contain your full name, title, company name and snail mail address.

Example   Brant Tymko, Director of Traffic Flow
Universal Securities Inc.
2345 Second Street
Halifax NS B3L 1G2
(902) 325-6489 Fax (902) 325-6401

A signature box on a message that is going to someone within your organization should contain your name and phone number. Your title is optional.

Example   Brant Tymko
325-6489

12. Disclaimers can protect senders and their companies from legal implications (copyright infringement, invasion of privacy, formation of contracts, etc.) resulting from emails — or at least reduce the risk. Most messages do not need them. However, many organizations, particularly financial institutions, have them added automatically to any email sent by an employee. If you are not sure whether your organization adds a disclaimer automatically, then send an email to yourself and check whether the information has been added.

There is no clear-cut answer as to whether all emails actually need disclaimers. My guideline is "if in doubt, use one." If your company does not have a formal policy on the wording of disclaimers, you will find some suggestions in Sample 18. (You can add the information to your signature box, two or three lines under your contact information.) If you have serious concerns about this issue, consult your lawyer. I believe that the more paranoid the company, the longer the disclaimer.

Please note that disclaimers cannot protect the sender from any libelous statements. Be careful about what you write by email.

SAMPLE 18
EXAMPLES OF DISCLAIMERS

1. This email is intended for the original recipient only.

2. This email is confidential and is only intended for the individuals authorized to receive it. If you are not the intended recipient, please notify the sender and do not read, copy, use or disclose the contents, but instead, please delete the message and any copies.

3. The contents of this email may be privileged and confidential. It may not be disclosed to or used by anyone other than the addressee(s), nor copied in any way. If received in error, please advise the sender, and then delete it from your system.

4. This email is private and confidential to the named recipients. Any information provided is given in good faith. However, unless specifically stated to the contrary, STARBRIGHT accepts no liability for the content of the email, or of the consequences of any actions taken on the basis of the information provided, unless that information is subsequently confirmed in writing. The unauthorized copying of any information contained in this email to persons other than the named recipients is strictly forbidden.

5. The information in this email is confidential, privileged and is subject to copyright. It is intended solely for the addressee(s) named. Access to this email by anyone else is unauthorized. If you are not the intended recipient, any disclosure, copying or distribution is prohibited and may be unlawful. When addressed to our clients, any information contained in this email is subject to the terms and conditions expressed in any applicable agreement governing the use of STARBRIGHT services.

6. This email is intended only for the person or entity to which it is addressed and may contain information that is confidential. If you are not the addressee indicated in this message (or responsible for delivery of the message to such person), you may not copy or deliver this message to anyone. Please destroy this message and notify me by email. Please advise immediately if you or your employer does not consent to email for messages of this kind. Opinions, conclusions and other information in this message that do not relate to the official business of STARBRIGHT shall be understood as neither given nor endorsed by it.

EMAIL ETIQUETTE

13. Think twice before forwarding information to a third party without the permission of the sender. Ask yourself whether the information is sensitive or involves copyright.

14. Use receipts carefully. Some people find it irritating when a writer asks for an electronic "have read" notice. By the way, when you receive a "have read" notice, it does not mean that your message was read and understood. It merely means that it was opened.

15. Never "chew" anyone out online. Emails have an extremely long shelf life. Even if you erase a message, it may still exist on your server, on the receiver's server, and in the receiver's sent box or other files. Be careful about what you say.

16. Never write anything you would not want seen on the front page of a newspaper. Emails can be used in lawsuits.

17. Think twice before sending a message to a group of people. Only send copies of your message to people who you know will want or need to receive it.

18. Avoid humor and sarcasm. They don't work well in emails. If you want to be funny, do it when you meet face to face. Then you can truly judge the receiver's response.

19. Use appropriate punctuation and capitalization. Never send a message in all capital letters, as this implies that you are yelling. Sending a message in all lowercase letters is also considered unprofessional.

20. Erase unneeded material below your message. No one likes long, unnecessary threads.

21. Be careful about color on messages. It can be distracting. Many readers dislike receiving messages with wallpaper (a colored background) on them because they can be hard to read. In addition, if receivers reply, the color of the response font changes to a color that may not show up well against the original wallpaper. For example, if you receive a message with a white font on a deep purple background, your reply will turn into black print on deep purple and will be hard to view. You will then have to change the background color or turn it off. This seems like a lot of unnecessary work. A manager once told me, "If my people have time to put color into their messages, they don't have enough work to do."

22. Tell the reader in the body of the email what they will find in an attachment. Readers find it irritating to receive an attachment without any explanation of why they should open it.

23. Limit emoticons or smileys. Although these "happy faces" were in vogue a few years ago, they are now deemed unprofessional in the business world. Save them for your personal messages.

24. Be careful with acronyms. Use them only if you are positive the reader understands them. Some short forms such as LOL can confuse readers. For example, LOL can refer to "laughing out loud" or "lots of love." The shorthand that we are becoming accustomed to in text messaging (e.g., *u* for *you*) is not considered appropriate in business emails.

25. Use abbreviations as long as you are sure the reader will understand them.

26. Place any social chitchat at the end of your message — if you are someone who enjoys the social niceties. Don't start with it, as some readers find this annoying.

27. Protect yourself against an email break-in. Never give away your password, and update it on a regular basis.

28. When passing a colleague's desk, don't look at the emails on the computer screen, unless you are invited to do so.

29. Check your subject line before you hit the send key. Does the subject line reflect the message? If the email is one that has had comments added to it over time by a number of people, chances are that the original subject doesn't fit. Change it.

30. Run spell-check before sending messages. Obvious spelling errors will detract from your professional image.

31. Use spelling that will be familiar to your reader, so you won't distract the reader from your message. For example, use US spelling for American readers. Also, use internationally recognizable dates, times, and measurements when appropriate.

SURVIVING YOUR READER'S INBOX

Most business people receive so many emails a day (some of them completely irrelevant to them and their work) that sorting them becomes quite a task. When you look at your inbox — if you are like most business readers — you start to prioritize which emails can be deleted, which must be opened immediately, and which ones can sit a while longer before you open them.

How do you make these decisions? First, most people check the name of the person who sent the message. If the message is from their manager or from a person they are waiting to hear from, they open these messages immediately. Second, they look at the subject line. If the subject lines appeal to them, they open these emails next. Third, they look at the opening line to see if the message applies to them. If fact, some people set their computers on preview mode, so they can review the opening lines and decide what to do with the message without even opening the email. If it is of little interest, they may delete the message without reading it.

Therefore, if you want your emails read and acted upon quickly — and you are not a VIP to the reader — you need to make sure your subject line and your opening paragraph gets "buy-in" from the reader.

SUBJECT LINES

32. Always have a subject line. Some readers automatically delete messages that don't have subject lines, assuming that they are spam.

33. Write descriptive subject lines. Depending on your font size, you have anywhere from 45 to over 100 spaces to use. Help your reader prioritize to your message.

34. Use priority flags on your messages, but recognize that, as these have been abused over the past few years, many readers ignore them.

35. Start your subject line with indicators that highlight the importance of the message. The following are some commonly used indicators:

   • RE: (meaning "I am responding to your question.")

   • URGENT (meaning "This message is time critical.")

   • FYI (meaning "This is for your information only. No reply required.")

   • REQ. (meaning "Please read, as action is required.")

   Examples   FYI: Your car lights have been left on

   URGENT: Computer problem is impacting customers

36. If you have a critical deadline, include it in both the subject line and the body.

Example   (*subject line*)

REQ: Information for Alliance contract req'd Sept. 6

(*body*)

The Alliance proposal is due next week. I would appreciate it if you could send me your input by Sept. 6, so that I can include it.

37. Never send one- or two-word emails. It is a waste of time for a receiver to open a message only to find the words *Thank you*. One alternative is to type the words *Thank you* or a short message in the subject line followed by the words *END*, or *EOM* (end of message), or NT (no text). This gets the point across, and tells the reader that there is no need to open the message.

Example   (*subject line*)

Thank you for the information   EOM

OPENING LINES

Readers determine whether or not to spend time on your email by the first paragraph. They then continue to read until they become bored or think that they have understood your message. That's why an email cannot be organized in the same fashion as a letter. In a hard copy letter, you know that the receiver will likely read the top paragraph and the bottom paragraph. In an email, you can only be guaranteed they will read the opening paragraph.

38. Place your reason for writing and your action request (or the thought you want to leave in your reader's mind) in the first paragraph. See Samples 19 and 20 for examples of a poorly organized message and a revised one.

39. Use the inverted pyramid approach to writing: move from the most important idea to the least important. Action requests should never appear at the end of a message, as the reader may not get there.

SAMPLE 19
AN EMAIL WRITTEN IN LETTER STYLE (POOR)

(This message is written in a letter style. It is too lengthy, confusing, filled with spelling errors and written in an outdated, pompous style. Also, the last paragraph is inappropriate and negates the actual message. See Sample 20 for a rewrite.)

(Nothing in subject line or greeting line)

Some of you are acutely aware that our nearly complete transition from the historical reliance on ABC systems, database and accounting practice to our new self-directed organization and processes has not been all smooth sailing. One of the most difficult challenges for our acounting group has been reconciling our accounts to the complex intracacies of the ABC Oracle database. REconciling the accounts is a top priority as those of you who teach FOF will know, and it has syphoned resources away from other important tasks.

As experienced practitioners and change agents I am sure you sympathize with the realities of what we are going throught.

Unfortunately, one of the outcomes of the transition has been a less than acceptable timeliness in processing some of your invoices. Those of your who have inquired/complained have every right to do so and I apologize on behalf of all of us for late payment.

I can insure you that this is not our expected future service level. In fact, our future service standard for faculty invoice turnaround will be 20 days.

If their remain any outstanding invoices that are in excess of 30 days at present, kindly inform me by email and provide the details and I will expedite as best I can.

Paul Smithers
Vice President Development

SAMPLE 20
MESSAGE REWRITTEN IN EMAIL FORMAT

Vendors,

We apologize for the late processing of your invoices over the past few months. Moving our accounting information to a new package created a number of unexpected problems. However, the problems are licked, and we are back to business as usual.

Now that the new package is up and running correctly, you will find that our accounts payable department operates efficiently and effectively.

If there is anything else you want to bring to our attention, please contact me directly. I would be happy to hear from you.

Thank you,

Paul Smithers
Vice President Development
416-345-5678

---

40. Remember that everyone listens to the radio station WII-FM (What's in it for me). If you start your email with a "what's in it for them" opening ("me" being the reader), you will get a faster response.

    Example Weak: Please send us your invoice by Friday.

    Better (*Using WIIFM technique*):

    If you send us your invoice by Friday, we will be able to pay you by the end of the month.

41. Appeal to the reader's better nature. This is another technique for getting reader buy-in in the opening paragraph.

Example Weak: Please answer this email from a client.

Better (*Appealing to the reader's better nature*): With your expertise in this area, you are probably better able to help this customer than I am. Would you mind replying to him directly?

42. If you cannot use either the WIIFM or the appeal technique, give a reason for your email in the opening paragraph.

Example Weak: We have revised the parking lot. Here is your new space.

Better (*Giving a reason*): For safety reasons, we have added new lights to the parking lot. Unfortunately, this has forced us to reorganize the lot. Here is your new space.

See Samples 21 and 22 for additional examples of a poorly organized message and a revised one.

Use Checklist 4 to check if you're using the best tone, style, and format for your emails.

SAMPLE 21
POOR EMAIL

(This email doesn't work. The focus is on the writer, not the reader. It is visually intimidating, and it takes too long for the reader to find out why he or she needs to read this document. See Sample 22 for a rewrite.)

Joe, Last week I attended the Corporate Communications Conference in Toronto. As usual it was a highly informative event, attracting over 800 professional communicators from across North America. The organization has been meeting for ten years now and is focused on improving internal and external communications in large companies. The conference format is to have three leading media specialists as keynoters and many other experts doing the concurrent sessions. They change the venue every year.

When I arrived at the conference, I ran into Lucy Chin, Margaret Mackay (from head office) and Arbi Satourni. (You might remember Arbi from last year's sales conference.) We decided that because of the wide number of concurrent sessions, we should divide the conference between the three of us and share the information afterwards. We again divided the information on the morning of the second day. On the afternoon of the second day, we met in a small conference room to discuss our ideas.

Something that became very clear is that we should improve the …

SAMPLE 22
MESSAGE REORGANIZED FOR EMAIL DELIVERY

Joe,

We are having problems with both internal and external written communications throughout the organization, and I believe we need a comprehensive writing program. Because of your expertise in this area, I'd like to get your input on the following six recommendations we want to put before senior management.

If you find it faster, please embed your answers with the recommendations.

We recommend:

1. Setting up a team to review an extensive sampling of the reports and correspondence produced by each department (The team should work with senior managers on an individual basis to determine their perceptions of areas for improvement.)

2. Designing a workshop specifically tailored for our staff.

3. Meeting with senior managers in a group setting to outline the workshop's agenda and to explain key objectives. (The workshop can still be fine-tuned at this point.)

4. Instructing managers on the combined art of editing and coaching so that they can provide constructive feedback.

5. Encouraging managers to attend the workshop with their staff.

6. Having the program announced by a high-ranking executive to give it proper weight. (The announcement should stress the purpose and importance of the program.)

These recommendations were put together by Lucy Chin, Margaret Mackay, Arbi Satourni, and me after last week's Corporate Communications Workshop in Toronto.

Thank you for your help.

Susan Sheridan
519-234-4567 ext. 210

CHECKLIST 4
EMAILS

After you have composed your email, ask yourself:

- ☐ Did I think about my reader before I composed the message?
- ☐ Is an email the right method for communicating this particular message?
- ☐ Is the subject line descriptive and interesting?
- ☐ Is there a deadline involved? Did I include this information in the subject line and in the body?
- ☐ Did I start with a greeting?
- ☐ Does the first paragraph tell the reader why he or she should read the document?
- ☐ Did I include only the pertinent details and omit everything else?
- ☐ Did I use the inverted pyramid approach for delivering the information?
- ☐ Did I keep the paragraphs short — under five lines in the body and two to three lines in the opening and closing paragraphs?
- ☐ Did I leave a blank line between paragraphs?
- ☐ Did I use lists to convey a series of ideas?
- ☐ Are the names, dates, times, and figures accurate?
- ☐ Did I type the message in upper- and lowercase, and use the correct punctuation?
- ☐ Did I end with a closing line?
- ☐ Did I include a signature box?
- ☐ Have I allowed the righthand side of the type to run ragged?
- ☐ Are there any spelling errors?
- ☐ Did I try to reduce the number of attachments?
- ☐ Am I sending this message only to the people who need to receive it?

Chapter 7

20 TIPS FOR WRITING SHORT REPORTS AND MEMOS THAT GET READ AND ACTED UPON

Short reports present wonderful opportunities for getting you noticed by both colleagues and senior management. They can be used to convey or update information, solve problems, make recommendations, or propose a new service or idea. They are normally one to ten pages in length.

Short reports have a variety of window dressing treatments. They can be written in memo style with a *To, From, Date,* and *Subject* line; they can have a title at the top of a page; or they can have a formal title page. Some even include a table of contents. (The setup for memo-style short reports is discussed in the Window Dressing section of this chapter.)

Regardless of the introductory set up or the window dressing, short reports must be visually appealing so that they do not intimidate the reader. To ensure that your documents get read, keep them as short as possible and use every possible technique for good communication:

- Subheads to break up long portions of text

- Short paragraphs

- Lists (with numbers, bullets, or dashes)
- White space

Many businesses have replaced short memos with emails. (For information on how to convey information in an email format, refer to Chapter 6.)

Here are some additional guidelines for the preparation of short reports.

ORGANIZATION

1. Think about the information you need to convey. Is a short report the best means of communication? Could the message be delivered better face to face or by phone? If the message is sensitive, think twice before you commit it to paper. Can you risk having others read this information? How would you feel if your document was released to the press? In today's world, very little can be kept confidential. If you must record your message, take care that it cannot be misinterpreted.

   On the other hand, if there are several people who need to receive the information, would a short report be more efficient than a verbal explanation to each of these people? If so, go ahead and write your message.

   If you are not happy with the quality of your short reports, or if you believe that you spend too much time writing them, try using Worksheet 3 to organize your thoughts.

2. There are four types of short reports you might have to write. Each type has its own organizational format, outlined in Table 8.

   (a) The information short report is used to deliver or request information or to ask for assistance (see Sample 23).

   (b) The problem-solving short report suggests specific actions to improve a situation (see Sample 24).

   (c) The persuasion short report is for occasions when you want to encourage the reader to undertake an action he or she doesn't have to take (see Sample 25).

(d) The internal proposal memo conveys suggestions to senior management (see Sample 26).

WORKSHEET 3
PLANNING TOOL FOR SHORT REPORTS

1. Fill in the blanks to describe your reason for writing this particular short report.

I am writing to (*supply verb*) _____

(*who*) _____ about

(*what*) _____

If you have trouble filling in these spaces, the following lists may help you.

Verb (why you are writing)	Who (who will read it)	What (what you are writing about)
inform	my boss	a new idea
persuade	my staff	a new procedure
recommend	colleagues	information
solve a problem	council/board	decision
provide an update	my department	results of a meeting
request	my organization	permission
instruct		a new policy
document		personnel problem
alert		assistance

2. List the key points you must cover in the short report.

_____

_____

3. Record the action you want the reader to take after reading your short report.

_____

_____

4. Now, arrange this information according to the short-report formats listed in Table 8, and begin to write.

TABLE 8
FORMATS FOR WRITING SHORT REPORTS

TYPE OF SHORT REPORT			
Information	**Problem-solving**	**Persuasion**	**Internal Proposal**
Main idea	State the problem	Begin with an agreeable point	Reason for writing
Expand on details	Analyze it	Introduce the idea	Outline present situation and state your proposal
Action required	Make a recommendation	State benefits to the reader	
		Action required	Describe advantage(s)
		Call to action	Mention and defuse disadvantage(s)
			Call to action

WRITING

3. Follow the rules for good writing listed in Chapter 3.

4. Keep your message brief and simple. Specify the actions the reader should take.

5. If you are making a recommendation, don't include only the positive details; include the drawbacks and defuse them yourself. Otherwise, readers may think you haven't researched the topic thoroughly.

> **Example** Although implementing the new system will decrease our productivity for several weeks, the long term benefits of greater accuracy and speed outweigh this concern.

FORMAT FOR INFORMATION SHORT REPORT

February 3, 20--

To: Maggie Maloney, Bob Arthur, and Evan Sharp

From: Mark Swierszcz

Re: Planning for September 17–18 Sales Conference

Main idea

It's time to start organizing the annual sales conference again. If the four of us could get together next week, we can begin planning the agenda and dividing the workload.

By starting now, the event will be highly successful, and no one will end up handling a lot of last-minute details.

Details

The following is a list of proposed dates and times. Let me know which dates fit your schedule and I will set up a meeting convenient for everyone.

February 11: 9:00–11:30 a.m.

February 12: 1:30–4:00 p.m.

February 13: 8:00–10:30 a.m.

Expected action

Please get back to me by Friday.

SAMPLE 24
FORMAT FOR PROBLEM-SOLVING SHORT REPORT

Date: October 24, 20--

To: All Transit Staff (permanent and part-time)

From: Chris Selvam, Transit Planner

Subject: Guidelines for Sharing Workstations

State the problem

We are having a problem with our public image. Some members of the public have complained about receiving inaccurate information from our staff regarding bus routes and construction detours.

Analysis

Part of the problem is caused by different shifts sharing the same workstations. If new information is not posted, the next shift is unaware of changes.

Problem

A related problem concerns the cleanliness of the workstations. This is particularly true on the weekends when the cleaning staff is unavailable.

Recommendation

To remedy both these concerns, before you leave at the end of your shift please —

- Display new information in an easily accessible spot.

- Remove outdated information.

- Tidy your station.

- Remove all personal hygiene items.

- Replace all items borrowed from other workstations.

- Empty your green recycling folder.

- Return dirty dishes to the cafeteria.

- Empty the fridge.

SAMPLE 25
FORMAT FOR PERSUASION SHORT REPORT

Date: April 14, 20--

To: All staff

From: Aurora Borealis

Re: Interim Place Annual Campaign

Agreeable point

The staff of Mahood, Rubincam, and Gallant have always had a proud tradition of supporting Interim Place. This is an excellent organization dedicated to providing food and shelter to the needy in our city.

Introduction of idea

Soon, you will be able to share in this fine tradition once again, through your support of the annual campaign.

Benefit to reader

By donating just one hour's pay per month, through payroll deduction, you can help ensure the human-care needs of our city are met for the upcoming year.

Action required if reader accepts

Next week, you will receive a payroll deduction form with your paycheck. Please check off your donation and return it to:

> Paul McLeod
> Payroll Office
> 5th Floor

Call to action

I urge you to join me in contributing to Interim Place so together we can help improve the quality of life for the less fortunate.

SAMPLE 26
FORMAT FOR INTERNAL PROPOSAL MEMO

Date: May 4, 20--

To: Todd O'Brien, President

From: Bronwyn McLeod, Administrative
          Manager

Subject: Improving the Appearance of Cobden
          Corp.'s External Correspondence

Reason for writing

It is important the external correspondence produced by Cobden Corp. reflect the professionalism of our organization. Currently, we do not have a specific style guide. Although all of the staff do use letterhead, they choose whatever font, type size, margins, and letter setup they wish.

Present situation

This individualized approach gives many of our documents an unprofessional — and at times sloppy — appearance. In addition, when several of us are writing to the same client, we do not present the image of a unified group.

Proposal

I recommend management arrange to have a style guide produced and distributed to all employees. I am sure there is someone on staff who could undertake this project. It should not be a time-consuming process.

Advantages of proposal

In addition, many of our engineers are now typing their own documents, and they have not been trained in standard keyboard practices. This guide will assist them in their work, answer any style questions, and ensure all of Cobden Corp.'s documents have a more professional and consistent appearance.

Disadvantages
of proposal
and rebuttal

Although our staff are used to "doing their own thing" in terms of correspondence, and some may prefer not to use the style selected, the clients' perception of our company is an important issue. We are trying to build a name for ourselves as an experienced team of hard-working, skilled people. I believe a style guide will contribute to this image.

Call to
action

Please let me know if you would like me to assign someone to this task, or if you wish to discuss it further at the weekly meeting.

6. Omit irrelevant words and information. Don't waste readers' time by making them sift through unimportant facts. Not only could this be confusing, but it may provide readers with details suggesting a conclusion or an act you did not intend.

   Ask yourself what the point, sentence, or phrase contributes to the message. If it adds little or nothing, eliminate it.

7. The tone of a short report can range from semiformal to informal depending on the reader and the occasion. Naturally, a short report to your manager set up as a memo would be less formal than a report with a cover page sent to a client.

8. Short reports can be written in point-form style rather than narrative when dealing with —

   • an existing client who does not require extensive background information,

   • one reader who does not have any personal style issues,

   or

   • information you want to deliver in a casual manner.

WINDOW DRESSING

9. Most short reports have a cover page including the name of the report, the writer, and the date of submission. If the report is over seven pages, you might want to use the second page for a short table of contents.

10. The memo setup is used only for written communication within an organization. The most common memo starts off with the following information:

    Date:
    To:
    From:
    Subject: *or* Re:

    The exact order of these headings may change depending on the company's official style. Some organizations have letterhead printed in memo form; others provide generic forms to simplify and standardize the information. If your organization does not have a specific form, use the common memo setup.

11. The date is the date the memo is written. Even though this is an informal type of communication, spell out the month. Do not use abbreviations — it makes you look unprofessional. Avoid using numbers for months and days unless this is your company's policy. Numbers can cause confusion.

12. The *To:* and *From:* lines carry the names of the writer and the intended reader. Whether you use *Mr.* or *Ms.* depends on the culture of the organization and the person to whom you are writing. Job titles and department names are often omitted if the sender and receiver know each other well. However, if you believe this memo might serve as a future record, include titles.

    If the memo is sent to more than one person, it may be possible to fit two or three names beside or under the *To:* line.

    Examples To: Jennifer Becevello, Susan Blakey, and Shannon McTaggart *or*

To: Jennifer Becevello
    Susan Blakey
    Shannon McTaggart

If it is not possible to fit the names of the addressees in the *To:* area, use the phrase: *See distribution list.* At the end of the memo, type the word *Distribution,* leave one line blank, and then list the names of the people who will receive a copy of the memo. Arrange the names by rank, department, or alphabet. (See Sample 27.) If space is tight, use two or more columns.

Be careful who you put on your distribution list. Ensure that the memo goes out to everyone who needs to read it, but don't over distribute. If someone doesn't need the information or doesn't want it, take them off your list. Don't use a memo merely to blow your own horn. If you have any doubts about whether or not memos should go to a particular person, ask.

13. Include a *Copy to:* line at the bottom of the memo if you want to alert someone to the information but don't expect him or her to carry out the same action as the people listed on the To: line or in the distribution list. Be sure, however, that there is a good reason for copying the person. Don't do it merely because you want the reader to think you're a busy employee.

14. Memos should announce their purpose in the *Subject:* or *Re:* line. The subject line should be specific and should instantly give readers enough information to know why they are reading it. It can be two lines long, if required.

Example   New Procedure

Better   New Procedure for Submitting Expense Accounts — Effective Immediately

15. Keep in mind the message should stand by itself and should not rely on the subject line. Do not use the term *above-mentioned.* If you do, the readers' eyes will immediately go back and check the subject line. Then they must come back and find the spot where they left off reading. Don't be lazy. Type out the word or phrase again.

INFORMATION MEMO WITH DISTRIBUTION LIST

Date: July 28, 20--

To: See distribution list

From: Ms. Grace Kiers, Medical Staff Secretary

Re: Ethics Committee Meeting Scheduled for
September 10, 20--

The first Ethics Committee meeting of the fall season has been scheduled for Tuesday, September 10, 20--, at 1600 hours in the hospital boardroom.

A regular monthly meeting time will be decided at this meeting.

Distribution list

Dr. David Clarkson, Chair

Ms. Connie Day, Medical Admin.

Mr. Michael Day, Community Rep.

Dr. Anthony Donohoe, Psychology

Mr. Marc Doucet, Religious Services

Ms. Victoria Glassford, Social Work

Ms. Suzanne Watson, Nursing

Dr. James Skipper, Surgery

Dr. Natalia Lobach, Obstetrics

Dr. Michael Zajdman, Pediatrics

Example   With regard to the above-mentioned project, ...

Better   With regard to the Rainbow Ridge project, ...

Note: Do not use the phrases *in regards to* or *with regards to*. The correct terms are *in regard to, with regard to, as regards,* or *regarding.*

16. If your reader is not familiar with the subject or with the background of the problem being dealt with, outline it in the opening paragraph. This introduction will provide necessary information months or even years later. The introductory paragraphs in follow-up memos should be shorter and, if necessary, can reference the background information included in the earlier memo.

Example   Here is the May update on the Rainbow Ridge project. (Background information on this project is available in the memo of January 17, 20--.)

17. Use plenty of white space. Remember you have to make the page appear visually attractive so the receiver is encouraged to read it.

18. Include subheads to organize the text into manageable bites of information, call attention to key ideas, and signal topic changes. Whenever possible, number points and put series of ideas in a list form.

19. Memos are written communications within an organization. Therefore, they do not have a complimentary close such as *Thank you* or *Thanking you in advance, Yours truly,* or *Sincerely.* Close with the action you wish the reader to take.

Examples   I look forward to your response by July 3.

Please file this information in the Policy and Procedures Manual.

As soon as you send me the figures, I'll complete the proposal.

20. Memos must be signed to indicate they were actually composed by the person listed on the *From:* line. Writers

may sign their names in full at the end of the memo or initial their names on the *From:* line. As the name — and the title, if necessary — appears at the top of the memo, it should never be repeated at the bottom.

After you have written your short report or memo, evaluate it using Checklist 5.

CHECKLIST 5
SHORT REPORTS AND MEMOS

After you have written a short report, ask yourself:

☐ Did I analyze the reader and his or her needs before I began to write?

☐ Is a short report/memo the best method for communicating my message?

☐ Does the subject line adequately describe the memo's purpose?

☐ Is my tone appropriate to the reader?

☐ Will the reader easily understand the words and jargon I used?

☐ Did I eliminate all unnecessary words and ideas?

☐ Did I keep it as short as possible but include all relevant information?

☐ Did I use a variety of sentence lengths?

☐ Did I use lists whenever possible?

☐ Is there plenty of white space?

☐ Did I follow the appropriate format?

☐ If I require specific action from the reader, did I close with this request?

☐ Did I include any necessary dates?

☐ Is this the sort of document I am proud to sign?

☐ Would I be embarrassed if this document were released to the media now or in the future?

Chapter 8

37 WAYS TO TAKE THE STRESS AND DRUDGERY OUT OF REPORT WRITING AND MAKE YOUR REPORTS READABLE

Reports play a significant role in business. When you are asked to write one, consider it an investment in your career. After all, anyone who can express new ideas, solutions, and analyses in a clear, concise fashion is always in demand. View your reports as a forum for expression and a chance to shine.

A report is not complicated. It is merely a collection of information, arranged in a particular format, and prepared by an expert. And you, the writer, are the expert.

Does this sound overwhelming? It shouldn't. You communicate orally on the job all the time. A written report is nothing more than an effective summary of the knowledge you have, or the information you can discover, about the area under consideration.

Reports come in a variety of shapes and sizes. They can run anywhere from one page (short report) to an indefinite number of pages (scientific report). They can be laid out in a variety of formats: memorandum, letter, semiformal, or formal.

Reports are essential tools for management, especially when they are conceived and prepared properly. Good reports give the reader answers, or at least ideas. They are also —

- objective,
- research-based,
- backed by graphics, when possible, and
- written in a clear, concise style.

However, it isn't enough just to provide basic information to your readers and expect them to interpret it. Recipients of reports often claim they are frustrated because reports list information but do not solve problems. Remember, a good report writer gives answers as well as information.

Other complaints associated with reports relate to poor organization of details, weak statements designed to protect the writer, and missed deadlines.

The following tips are designed to help you prepare timely, effective reports that meet the readers' needs.

1. How do you eat an elephant? The answer: one bite at a time. Reports are the same. They can be overwhelming — particularly formal reports. However, if you divide the process into smaller steps, such as the ones listed below, it will ensure your final product is one you can be proud of.

    Here are six steps for successful report writing:

    (a) Analyze the reader and the purpose

    (b) Gather the details

    (c) Organize the information

    (d) Write

    (e) Rest

    (f) Edit and revise

    It has been proven that people who spend 40 percent of their time on the first three stages, 20 percent on the writing, and 40 percent on the editing, prepare better reports than people who spend 80 percent of their report preparation time on the actual writing.

If you are writing draft after draft after draft before you are happy with your report, chances are you are not spending enough time with the analyzing, gathering, and organizing stages.

STEP 1 — ANALYSIS

2. The first step in writing any document is, of course, getting to know your reader. Go back and complete Worksheet 1, Planning Tool for Reader Analysis, in Chapter 2.

   You should also identify the secondary audience. The secondary audience consists of people who may be sent copies of your document after the primary readers have reviewed it. For example, your immediate boss requests a report and, after reading it, sends it on to the supervisor, senior management, the board of directors, or council. It may even be made available to the news media and the public.

   Knowing where your report might end up provides a focus for the content, the details to be included or eliminated, and the vocabulary level.

3. In the second step, you should develop a thorough understanding of why the report is needed and exactly what it is you are focusing on. This is an area many writers don't spend enough time on. Until you are clear on the *what* and the *why*, do not begin to write. This information affects the arrangement of the details, and if you haven't determined the *why* and the *what* up front, you will waste time writing and rewriting.

   The *why* usually falls into one of two areas. You are either providing information to the readers so they can make a decision or take specific action, or you are analyzing a situation and making a recommendation.

   Don't begin writing until you can reduce your purpose statement to two sentences. The statement does not have to be grammatically correct; no one but you will read it. (I like to write the statement on a file card and keep it in front of me while I am working on the report. This keeps me on track and reduces the possibility of detours into irrelevant details.)

Two writers were asked to prepare reports on the maintenance costs of their office's equipment. The manager was thinking of replacing some of the older machines. Each writer worked on a purpose statement and then proceeded with the report. Here are the results:

Writer One's purpose statement:
The purpose of this report is to assess the maintenance costs of the existing office equipment.

Writer Two's purpose statement:
The purpose of this report is to present and analyze the maintenance costs of the photocopier, printers, and personal computers in my department and recommend which machines should be replaced. I will also include the costs of replacement equipment and trade-in values.

Writer One spent less time on the purpose statement but a longer time writing the actual text of the report. That report was late and disorganized.

Writer Two spent more time on the purpose statement but less time actually writing. This report was on time and was well received because of the conciseness of the information and the recommendation.

STEP 2 — GATHERING THE DETAILS

4. Once you have focused on the reader and the purpose of the report, it is time to gather the details.* They will come from your own head, hard copy, electronic documents, or from discussions or interviews with concerned sources.

---

*Many professional writers use mindmapping techniques at this point to develop a more creative approach to their writing. Other names for similar techniques are brainstorming, clustering, branching, pressure writing, and webbing. They all involve bringing the subconscious mind into the writing process. We don't have room to examine these methods here, but two good books on this subject are *Mindmapping* by Joyce Wycoff and *Writing on Both Sides of the Brain* by Henriette Anne Klauser.

Remember, effective writers don't collect just the information that interests them. They collect the details their readers need and want.

STEP 3 — ORGANIZING THE INFORMATION

Once the facts have been gathered — and before you begin to write — organize the key points into a logical format.

Short reports

The organizational patterns for short reports are discussed in Chapter 7.

Formal reports

Formal reports are lengthy, contain complex information, involve research, and are written for upper management or external use.

5. Formal reports are divided into five sections:

   (a) Preliminary parts

     (i) Letter of transmittal

     (ii) Title page

     (iii) Contents page

     (iv) Executive summary or synopsis

   (b) Introduction

   (c) Body

   (d) Conclusions or summary

   (e) Addendums

     (i) Bibliography

     (ii) Appendix material*

     (iii) Index (if required)

---

*The appendix contains material that does not fit into the body of the report. It could include a glossary of technical terms, maps, complex mathematical formulas, survey instruments, or questionnaires. Be careful what you choose to include. Do not let this section be a dumping spot for the leftover details.

6. The letter of transmittal is the letter that accompanies the report. It serves the same purpose as an oral introduction would if you were to deliver the report in person. If the report is prepared for someone within your organization, the letter of transmittal may be written in a memo form.

   The letter of transmittal should —

   (a) begin with the purpose of the letter,

   (b) follow with an overview of the report (if the report includes a separate summary, keep this section brief),

   (c) acknowledge those who assisted with the study, and

   (d) thank the authority who requested the report for the opportunity to help.

   See an example of a letter of transmittal in Sample 28.

7. The title page should be as attractive as possible, as it is usually the first thing the reader sees (see Sample 29). It should include —

   (a) the comprehensive title,

   (b) the name of the person or authority who requested the report,

   (c) the author's name and organization, and

   (d) the date submitted.

8. The contents page, including page numbers, aids the reader who may want to read only certain parts of the report. It should contain each heading and subheading in the report.

   If there are more than five graphics in your report, list them in a separate section, titled *List of Figures*, after the contents page. List the name of the figure (table, graph, or chart) and the page number.

9. The executive summary or synopsis is a précis of the entire report. It is the one section you can be assured your audience will read. Keep it short and include only the highlights of the report (see Sample 30).

   Although it is one of the first items appearing in the report, you will find it easier if you write this section last.

SAMPLE 28
LETTER OF TRANSMITTAL

Dear Mr. Brown:

Here is the report you requested on the need for a central library in the town of Crystal.

To obtain this information, I conducted an opinion survey of 600 area residents. I also met with the staff of the three community libraries in the area to discuss their book collections, staffing, and space requirements.

The study indicates there is a definite need for a central library in Crystal.

The three head librarians and Ms. Marion Seymour of Technical Services were of particular help to me in organizing my research.

Thank you for the opportunity to conduct this study, Mr. Brown. It was both informative and enlightening. Please let me know if you would like to discuss this matter further.

Sincerely,

REPORT TITLE PAGE

The comprehensive title

The name of the person or authority who requested the report

The author's name and organization

The date submitted

An Analysis of the High School Dropout Patterns of Canadian Students

20--

Prepared for

The Department of Education

Prepared by

Julia Taush

and Jeffrey O'Brien

MW Consulting Services

July 12, 20--

EXECUTIVE SUMMARY

Executive Summary

On September 23, 20--, Rosehill Realty authorized a study to determine what type of restaurant is best suited for the northwest corner of Main and Sherbourne. This study was prompted by our appraisers, who have determined that this corner property has a best-use value as a location for a restaurant.

The study involved a survey of 500 people who live or work in the area of Main and Sherbourne. This number gives us a sufficient sample to represent the attitudes of the people who may use the restaurant.

The highlights of the study are:

(a) An almost equal number of people favor a restaurant with indoor and outdoor seating, or a fast-food service with indoor and outdoor seating.

(b) Eighty percent of the participants wish to pay less than $8 per lunch.

(c) A large number of participants (78%) spend less than 40 minutes eating lunch.

(d) A significant number of the people interviewed dine out several times a week.

(e) The meal most often eaten in a restaurant by the survey participants is lunch.

Based on these and other findings presented in the report, it is recommended that a fast-food chain, which provides indoor and outdoor seating, be approached to open a restaurant at this location.

10. Remember, the executive summary should include the following information:

    - The purpose of the document you are summarizing
    - Its most significant information
    - Its conclusions or results
    - Its recommendations or implications

11. An executive summary should not include:

    - Your own opinion and judgment, unless you are making recommendations
    - Information not included in the report
    - Irrelevant information
    - Background information
    - Remarks indicating that you are writing a summary (*This is a summary of ...* or *The author of this report states ...*)
    - Examples
    - References to anything in the original document (*See the graph on page 3.*)
    - Illustrations or tables

12. The introduction of a report should always cover the following areas:

    - Current situation
    - Alteration *(What's wrong with the current situation)*
    - Premise *(Your conclusion or recommendation)*
    - Specifics line *(What the reader will find in the report)*

    You don't have to write the information in this specific order. For example, if the situational details were extensive, you might start with the recommendation. If the problem will excite readers, you might begin with that. You just rearrange the connecting words and phrases.

    Note: The specifics line must always go last as it is the bridge between the introduction and the body of the report.

Example   Many companies have invested in computers and software packages to help their employees become more productive and efficient. *(Current situation)* However, staff are often too busy to fully explore how the various features can help them. *(Alteration)*

This is unfortunate as software programs, such as Microsoft Word and WordPerfect, have features that can assist people in becoming better writers. *(Premise)* This report outlines a plan for improving the productivity of our staff by training them on how to use their computers as writing tools. *(Specifics line)*

Example   Software programs, such as Microsoft Word and WordPerfect, have features that can assist people in becoming better writers. *(Premise)* However, staff are often too busy to fully explore how the various features can help them. *(Alteration)* This is unfortunate as many companies have invested in computers and software packages to help their employees become more productive and efficient. *(Current situation)*

This report outlines a plan for improving the productivity of our staff by training them on how to use their computers as writing tools. *(Specifics line)*

13. The body of the report explains how the facts lead to the conclusions or recommendations. This section is the most extensive part of the report and can be arranged in several ways, as shown in Table 9.

Graphics

14. Experts agree that most people get their information visually. Charts, tables, and graphs not only help your reader grasp what you are saying, but they also improve your ability to communicate complex ideas quickly and simply.

TABLE 9
METHODS OF ORGANIZING
INFORMATION REPORTS

Order of importance	List and discuss the most important idea first, then the second most important idea, and so on. The last point is the least important one.
Chronological	Arrange the events being discussed in sequential order, beginning with the first event and continuing on to the last.
Spatial	Describe an object or a process according to its physical arrangement or setting.
Step by step	Instruct the reader on how to carry out a specific activity.
Comparison	Compare items according to specific qualities.

15. On the other hand, some people are "chart blind." Give them a chart or a table and they will read all sorts of things into it. According to a Statistics Canada survey, one in five Canadians have trouble interpreting a line graph. A good tip is to tell people what they are going to see and then present them with the graphics.

Example   About two-thirds of the staff in our department have been with us for over eight years (see Figure 1).

Better   As shown in Figure 1, about two-thirds of the staff in our department have been with us for over eight years.

About two-thirds of the staff in our department have been with us for over eight years, as shown in Figure 1.

16. Under no conditions should a graphic be included in the report without being referred to in the text. Ideally, each graphic should come immediately after the text that mentions it. If the illustration is too big to come immediately after the text, it should appear on the page following, unless it is awkward to do so.

17. To avoid confusion, call each table, chart, or graph a *figure*, and number them sequentially. Don't forget to give each graphic a comprehensive title.

Getting ready to write

18. Once you have analyzed your reader, gathered the data, and picked the organizational pattern, fill in a storyboard planning sheet. Worksheet 4 is my favorite layout, but it can be easily modified to fit the needs of your specific report.

    These storyboard sheets are also beneficial when preparing a team report. Each member of the team fills in and works on the relevant portions of the sheet, and the group manager knows what to expect from every writer.

19. Seven is the magic number for writing reports. Never have more than seven main points. This is the limit for a reader's attention span. Likewise, never include more than seven sub-points for a main point. You may even go a level deeper into the report — to sub-sub points — but any level lower than that will only detract from the main points.

20. One of the major complaints about reports — from readers and writers — is that they are often not as well written as they should be because they are prepared under time constraints. To avoid a poorly written, or late, report, plan out your writing time before you start, working backwards from your due date.

    Worksheet 5 is a time sheet designed for writing reports. On the top line, record the various steps you need to take to prepare your report. In the left margin, record the various parts of the report. Then record the dates on which you intend to accomplish the specific areas. In the bottom of the boxes, fill in the dates when you actually complete that step. Now you can easily see how you are progressing, and will know when you can relax or when you have to step up the pace. Sample 31 shows this time sheet filled in for writing the first edition of this book.

WORKSHEET 4
STORYBOARD PLANNING TOOL FOR REPORTS

REPORT TITLE _____

FINAL DEADLINE _____

SECTION REQUIREMENTS

Point 1 _____

    Sub-point _____

    _____

    _____

    Graphic requirements _____

    Appendix requirements _____

Point 2 _____

    Sub-point _____

    _____

    _____

    Graphic requirements _____

    Appendix requirements _____

Point 3 _____

    Sub-point _____

    _____

    _____

    Graphic requirements _____

    Appendix requirements _____

Point 4 _____

    Sub-point _____

    _____

    _____

    Graphic requirements _____

    Appendix requirements _____

WORKSHEET 5
TIME SHEET

	Organize ideas	Write first draft	Edit first draft	Write second edit	Final edit

SAMPLE 31
TIME SHEET

	Organize ideas	Write first draft	Edit first draft	Write second draft	Final edit
Preface	Aug 31 / Aug 31	Aug 31 / Aug 31	Sept 5 / Sept 5	Sept 6 / Sept 6	Oct 7 / Oct 9
Chpt 1 Writing	Aug 16 / Aug 16	Aug 16 / Aug 16	Aug 17 / Aug 17	Aug 18 / Aug 18	Sept 20 / Sept 20
Chpt 2 Readers	Aug 21 / Aug 21	Aug 22 / Aug 21	Aug 29 / Aug 29	Aug 30 / Aug 30	Sept 21 / Sept 20
Chpt 3 Rules	June 30 / June 30	July 7 / July 6	July 12 / July 12	July 17 / July 13	Sept 22 / Sept 21
Chpt 4 Tone	July 17 / July 17	July 19 / July 19	July 20 / July 20	July 21 / July 22	Sept 25 / Sept 25
Chpt 5 Letters	July 24 / July 24	July 26 / July 26	July 27 / July 27	July 28 / July 28	Sept 30 / Sept 27
Chpt 6 Memos	July 31 / July 30	Aug 2 / Aug 1	Aug 3 / Aug 3	Aug 4 / Aug 4	Oct 2 / Oct 2
Chpt 7 Reports	Aug 8 / Aug 8	Aug 8 / Aug 8	Aug 10 / Aug 10	Aug 12 / Aug 12	Oct 3 / Oct 3
Chpt 8 Faxes and emails	Sept 6 / Sept 6	Sept 7 / Sept 7	Sept 8 / Sept 8	Sept 9 / Sept 13	Oct 5 / Oct 5
Chpt 9 Web writing	Aug 14 / Aug 14	Aug 15 / Aug 15	Aug 17 / Aug 17	Aug 18 / Aug 18	Oct 6 / Oct 6

STEP 4 — WRITING

21. When you are writing lengthy reports, you don't have to start at the beginning and work through to the end. If you have completed your storyboard sheet, you can start at any point you wish. Some people prefer to begin with the easiest sections and warm up to the harder ones. Others start with the most difficult.

22. Follow the normal rules for business writing discussed in Chapter 3.

23. Formal reports should be written with complete sentences, paragraphs, and headings. In addition, make sure you use full-length sentences when you know you will have multiple readers with different information needs.

24. Long paragraphs give the impression that the ideas expressed are important; short paragraphs imply less important thoughts. However, too many long paragraphs may intimidate some readers, as they call for more concentration. Try to reduce the number of paragraphs over eight lines in length.

25. Visual appeal is important in reports. Make sure you have plenty of white space, and leave ample margins in case the report is bound or placed in a binder. Some writers leave a wider margin on the right-hand side so readers can add their comments or questions in the appropriate places.

26. The tone in formal reports is objective and formal. Avoid the first person (*I* or *me*), and use more passive voice sentences than you would for letters, memos, and short reports.

27. Be prepared to make strong statements. Don't hedge when you take a stand; it makes you appear unprofessional and frustrates your readers.

    Example   Based on these figures, which I hope are accurate, it is recommended bidding be considered for the purchase of ABC company.

    Better   Based on these figures, I recommend Crystal Corporation purchase the ABC company.

28. Use the passive voice when presenting negative findings.

Example   You lowered morale in the office when you announced five people would be laid off.

Better   Morale in the office lowered when it was announced five people would be laid off.

29. Use active voice sentences when making recommendations.

Example   It is recommended that the new XYZ software package be purchased by the department.

Better   The committee recommends the department purchase the new XYZ software package.

30. If comparing two or more items, discuss them by the qualities being measured rather than by the items themselves (see Table 10).

31. Research shows that, with a long report, almost all readers will review the executive summary, a majority will read the introduction because it comes next, and then some will flip ahead and read the conclusion. Few will read the entire body of the report. Therefore, following Rules 32, 33, and 34 is essential.

32. In a long report, all major points should appear three times: in the body, in the executive summary, and in either the introduction or the conclusion or recommendation. Remember, few readers read a long report from cover to cover. By recording key points three times, there is a better chance that your audience will read those particular points.

33. Always reread the introduction after you have finished the entire report and make any necessary changes. Sometimes, in writing the body — even though you follow the outline you created before you began to write — you may add some extra details or take a slightly different slant than the one initially planned.

Make sure the introduction presents a concise picture of what is to follow. If it doesn't accurately reflect the upcoming ideas, your readers will be annoyed.

TABLE 10
ORGANIZATION FOR COMPARATIVE REPORTS

Example	Better
Introduction	*Introduction*
Site A	*Condition of existing buildings*
Condition of existing buildings	Site A
	Site B
Parking	Site C
Costs	
Site B	*Parking*
Condition of existing buildings	Site A
	Site B
Parking	Site C
Costs	
Site C	*Costs*
Condition of existing buildings	Site A
	Site B
Parking	Site C
Costs	
Recommendation	*Recommendation*
This method forces readers to flip back and forth between pages to understand the comparison.	This method presents the information in a format that is easier for the reader to evaluate.

34. Use descriptive subheads to deliver information to your readers. Keep in mind today's busy readers. Many will not take the time to thoroughly read a lengthy report, but they will skim the heads and subheads. Ensure that these titles are comprehensive and that they explain the gist of the information that follows.

   Example   By-elections

   Better   Rising costs of by-elections

35. In a long report, use a recognized numbering system and stick to it. Table 11 shows three basic systems you could use for your reports.

TABLE 11
NUMBERING SYSTEMS FOR REPORTS

Roman numeral	Alphanumeric	Decimal
I. (main point)	A.	1.0
A. (sub-point)	1.	1.1
1. (sub-sub point)	a.	1.1.1
2.	b.	1.1.2
B.	2.	1.2
II.	B.	2.0

STEP 5 — RESTING

36. Research indicates that writers do a better editing job if they rest at least two hours before beginning to edit their own writing. (Twenty-four hours is even better.) That way, you will be looking at the material with a slightly fresher, more objective, eye.

STEP 6 — EDITING

37. Editing is the key to all good reports. Forty percent of the report process should be spent in this stage. And remember to do a spell-check both manually and electronically. Checklist 6 gives you some questions to ask yourself.

CHECKLIST 6
EDITING REPORTS

After you have written your formal report, ask yourself:

☐ Does the title adequately describe the purpose of the report?

☐ Does the executive summary carry the significant highlights without overwhelming the reader with details?

☐ Does the introduction explain the purpose of the report?

☐ If it is a lengthy report, are all major points discussed three times in the appropriate sections?

☐ Did I include all the information the reader has to, and wants to, know? Did I omit everything else?

☐ Is the information arranged in a logical order?

☐ Are the figures, names, and dates accurate?

☐ Did I use the passive voice for negative findings and the active voice for recommendations?

☐ Is my report visually appealing?

☐ If my audience reads only the headings and subheadings, will they understand the gist of the report?

☐ Did I use a vocabulary level my primary readers will understand? My secondary readers?

☐ Did I write sentences that average 15–18 words and that require no more than four pieces of punctuation?

☐ Are the paragraphs less than eight lines long?

☐ Did I use lists when possible?

☐ Is the numbering system consistent?

☐ Did I use connecting words and phrases to move the reader through the material?

☐ Did I check for grammar errors or misused words?

Chapter 9

25 TIPS FOR BUILDING A BUSINESS CASE THAT INFLUENCES DECISION MAKERS

Every day, organizations face decisions about which project to fund — and competition for resources and funds is keen. This is where a good business case comes in. It "gets across" program needs with a businesslike approach and brings your ideas to life.

Some people call a business case a report or a proposal. However, a true business case varies from these documents because it answers the question "why."

All successful business documents answer a reader's questions. However, a recommendation report stresses the "what" — what the solution is to the reader's problem. A proposal answers the questions "who" and "how" — who will solve the reader's problem and how they will do it. A business case states "why" — why the reader is justified in spending money on this particular solution.

In other words, a business case is a tool that provides decision makers with all relevant information — including costs, benefits, and alternatives — so that they can make the appropriate decision on a potential change.

I call a business case a thinking person's tool. More than any other document, it requires careful thought before any information is put on paper.

This chapter looks at the various components of business cases and supplies the questions that should be considered before writing each section. Not all questions will apply to your particular document, but they may steer your overall thought processes onto a winning path.

THE READER

Business cases fail when they don't show how the reader can achieve his or her objectives. Therefore, the first step in deciding on whether to pitch your case is to consider your reader. In addition to reading Chapter 2, I suggest that you take time to answer these questions:

1. What is the reader's current objective? If your reader's current objective is to cut back on spending, now is not the time to bring forward a suggestion that will require additional funding.

2. What are the mission, vision, and values of the organization? Does your business case fit with these? It may help your cause if you can distinctly relate it to the organization's priorities.

3. What information does the reader already know? Dwelling too long on accepted facts wastes your reader's time and takes up too much space.

4. What questions will the reader have about your proposal? If you don't answer all of his or her questions, you may find your proposal is put on hold or turned over to a committee for further investigation. Once a proposal is handled by a committee, it seldom retains its original form.

5. Is your primary reader an expert or an executive? If he or she is an expert in the area you are discussing, place emphasis on jargon, research results, calculations, and formulas. If he or she is an executive, focus on the practical application and marketplace consequences of the business case.

If you have readers at both levels, then pitch the business case to the executive and include material in the appendix that will interest the expert.

THE TEMPLATE

Most organizations have their own template for a business case — some are quite lengthy; others are short. My own experience is that the majority of receivers don't have time to carefully read lengthy, complicated documents, and the higher a person is in the organization, the more this is true. Therefore, the shorter the business case — provided it carries all the relevant information — the more likely it is to get read and acted upon.

6. Here is a business case template that I find works very well:

   • Executive summary (if business case is lengthy)
   • Current state analysis
   • Solution/alternatives
   • Cost and benefit analysis
   • Risk Management
   • Implementation timetable
   • Conclusion and recommendation
   • Appendix

   The following discussion is based on this particular template. If your company's template is different, you may need to change the sequence in which you present the information.

EXECUTIVE SUMMARY

7. Information on writing an executive summary can be found in Chapter 8. Remember that although the executive summary appears first, it is the last piece to be written. Executive summaries are usually 10 percent or less of the original document's length.

CURRENT STATE ANALYSIS

8. A current state analysis differs from a standard background piece you would normally find in a report. It explains the driving factors behind the project/product/ solution (see the example that follows). The current state analysis should answer many of the following questions:

    (a) Why is your solution necessary?

    (b) What are the issues driving your solution? Address as many of the following topics as possible:

    - Operations
    - Assessment of technology
    - Clients/customers/public
    - Staff
    - Competitors
    - Trends in the marketplace

    Example   Our call center staff have always prided themselves on being able to contribute to service quality. Lately, however, they believe their ability to do so has been hampered by a lack of training and state-of-the-art tools. According to a recent internal survey, our employees are frustrated and believe that the organization no longer cares about them or about service quality. As their morale continues to decline, our customer satisfaction ratings have also dropped, as indicated in November's CSR form. In fact, for every 2 percent decrease in morale, we have seen a 6 percent decline in customer satisfaction.

SOLUTIONS/ALTERNATIVES

9. Once readers understand the driving forces behind your solution, they are then ready to hear your solution. A good business case also summarizes other solutions that were

considered. In addition, it should include a "do-nothing" scenario that stresses the implications to the organization if nothing is done.

10. A discussion of previously tried and failed efforts may also be appropriate if it helps justify why the solution you are proposing is required.

11. The amount of space you give to alternatives depends on the length of the business case your organization expects. If managers are looking for a hefty document, you would discuss the pros and cons of each alternative, and then provide the rationale for your final choice.

12. If you wish to prepare a shorter business case, you could discuss the alternatives briefly (see Sample 32). However, make sure you do mention them. If you don't, your reader may question the rationale for your recommendation.

COST AND BENEFIT ANALYSIS

The cost and benefit analysis is divided into two distinct areas: the costs of the solution and the benefits to the organization for incurring those costs.

Cost analysis

13. The cost section describes the costs associated with implementing the solution. Check with your finance division or controllers to get information on the methodology that is preferred for justifying financial expenditures. Use tables and graphs, where possible.

14. When considering the costs to be included, look at both implementation costs and recurring costs.

    In terms of implementation costs, look at the following:
    - Staffing
    - Equipment
    - Consultant's report
    - Operational support
    - Installation costs

SHORT SOLUTION/ALTERNATIVES SECTION

We recommend contracting with an office landscape company, Plants Indoors Inc., to handle our interior plant displays. Plants Indoors Inc. would provide technicians twice a month to water, feed, and trim all the plants in our building at 2345 Mississauga Road. This would include the displays in the main lobby, as well as all the plants in individual offices. The technicians would also clean all the plants and containers, and replace any plants that have deteriorated. The experienced technicians would work during standard business hours, and they have been trained to be unobtrusive.

We also considered asking our existing maintenance people to conduct these activities. However, these people are not trained in this field, and plant care was exempted from their contract during the last negotiation.

We could ask our own staff to maintain the plants in their offices and have the landscape company maintain only the displays in the main lobby. However, this is not a productive use of time, and few people have the expertise or tools to care for these plants. Replacing unhealthy plants might also be an issue.

As our organization initially paid close to $100,000 for the internal landscaping and have been using it as example of our environmentally friendly attitude, we believe that it is important that we maintain these displays. After meeting with three indoor landscape companies and evaluating their services according to experience, location, services, and costs, we recommend using the services of Plants Indoors Inc., which has a successful ten-year history with this type of work.

- Outsourcing costs

- Loss of productivity

- Any other operational impact costs

    When considering recurring costs, think about the following:

- Yearly costs to maintain the solution

- Standard maintenance, licensing, personnel, or supply costs

Benefits analysis

15. The benefits section describes the advantages associated with the solution. It is important that the benefits link back to the current state analysis and the key problems that initiated the business case.

16. Ask yourself whether there could be any benefits to the following:

- Operational savings

- Quality improvements

- Work volume reduction

- Customer or client satisfaction

- Revenue increases

- Increased market share

- Competitive position

- Positive public image

    Example   *Benefits* (business case for the purchase of a new voice mail system)

    Currently, some of our customers call the 800 order line whenever they call our organization. Unfortunately, this means that our order processing operators must locate the correct extension and transfer these calls to the appropriate persons. Not only does this take time, but it also irritates our customers.

The new, suggested process will utilize an automated call answering device permitting customers to select 1 to order products and 2 for customer service. This will reduce the volume of incorrect calls to the order operators. More important, it will project a more efficient image of our organization.

RISK MANAGEMENT

17. Spend time on the risk management section — particularly if a lot of money is involved. Readers want to be guaranteed that if they approve the solution, there is little chance of failure. A thorough discussion also shows that the writer has done his or her homework and has a plan in place if something should go wrong.

18. Although some people choose to do a SWOT (strengths, weaknesses, opportunities, and threats) analysis here, I find that too detailed, as it repeats many of the points listed previously.

    Since businesspeople prefer to have clear points that they can skim, I suggest using a chart that describes potential risks, the probability that they will occur, and any strategies that you will have in place to mitigate those risks (see Sample 33).

19. Remember to mention any risk the reader might consider to be a deterrent to your solution, and indicate whether it is actually a risk or not.

IMPLEMENTATION

20. The implementation section summarizes the key milestones and checkpoints. It makes the reader feel confident that you fully understand the project and will be able to control it. It also provides the reader with dates to confirm that the solution is being implemented on schedule. Therefore, don't underestimate the dates for your checkpoints; build in some time for unexpected delays.

RISKS SECTION FOR A BUSINESS CASE ON PURCHASING NEW SOFTWARE

Risks					
Risk Area	Description	Probability (1–4)	Impact (1–4)	Risk Ranking: High, Medium, Low	Current Risk Mitigation Strategies
Technical Complexity	Installation of software could disrupt our software or operating system.	1	1	Low	Installation will be scheduled on test environment first. Migration to development and production will occur after business hours. Installation will be completed within two hours.
Operational Impact	None				Installation will be scheduled after business hours.
External Customer Impact	None				Installation will be scheduled after business hours.
Starbright's Image	None				Installation will be scheduled after business hours.
Other					

21. Major steps to include could be the following:
    - Development
    - Testing
    - Training
    - Implementation
        - Change management activities
        - Educational activities
        - Major developmental steps
    - Communication, status meetings
    - Pilot programs
    - Rollout
    - Project wrap-up meeting

22. You can use a Gantt chart, or if you want to keep it simple, use Sample 34, a variation of the time sheets shown earlier. A Gantt chart is a popular type of bar chart that illustrates a project schedule.

CONCLUSIONS AND RECOMMENDATION

23. Some readers immediately skip to the end of a business case to get to the bottom line. Therefore, in this section restate key themes from each major section of the case. Include a summary of the issues, costs, and benefits of the solution. Then state your recommendation (see Sample 35).

FINAL THOUGHTS

24. Now that you have completed the necessary thinking behind a business case, you can move on to the actual writing. Remember to write clearly and concisely, as discussed in Chapter 3. Even though a business case is a high-level document, it requires an easy-to-read writing style to ensure that your readers quickly understand your key points.

SAMPLE 34
IMPLEMENTATION SECTION FOR A
BUSINESS CASE

Milestones	Date (estimated/ completed)	Who is responsible	Comments

CONCLUSIONS AND RECOMMENDATION

Conclusions

The purchase of scheduling software will help us to optimize our staff utilization and increase our staffing effectiveness. We will be the first extended health care provider in our region to use this tool, thus making us a leader in the field. In addition, we expect the time spent by our staff on schedule creation and management to reduce by 65 percent. We also expect our customer satisfaction level will increase from a 25 percent excellent rating to an 80 percent excellent rating, as we will be able to quickly place the appropriate healthcare worker in the right place at the right time.

It will take three months for the software to be loaded onto the laptops of 100 members of our staff. This will be done by our IT department, and the vendor will then follow up with the necessary training on our premises. We expect the number of client visits will be slightly reduced during the training period; however, this will be offset by the increased number of visits after the training period.

The area that will be impacted the most during the implementation phase will be the IT department. Some staff will be required to work during the weekend for three weeks to complete the installations.

The best provider of the scheduling and training packages is Kronos Schedulers, a proven name in providing this type of software. The cost for implementation would be $30,000 plus taxes.

Recommendation

Our staff were hired for their expertise in providing healthcare; however, they are currently spending time at our head office working on scheduling, referral, and organizing appointments with clients. The purchase of scheduling software will permit our staff to spend more time on their primary job responsibilities, free up office and parking space at head office, and provide our clients with the attention they deserve. I recommend that we purchase the Kronos Scheduling Software during our fourth quarter.

25. Make your document look visually appealing. Business cases can appear overwhelming, so keep your paragraphs short, insert plenty of subheadings, and use bulleted lists and charts when appropriate.

When you have prepared a business case, use Checklist 7 to ensure that you have adjusted the key points discussed in this chapter.

CHECKLIST 7
BUSINESS CASES

☐ Did I clearly identify my reader's needs and objectives before writing?

☐ Will my business case answer my reader's needs and objectives?

☐ Does the current state analysis identify the driving forces behind my proposal?

☐ Did I mention other alternatives to my solution, including the impact of not adopting a solution?

☐ Did I explain why choosing the alternatives or remaining with the status quo is not a good idea?

☐ Do my estimates include implementation costs and recurring costs? Are there any staffing implications?

☐ Did I consider all the risks that both the reader and I will find important?

☐ Did I point out the ways that I will mitigate any risks so that they will not endanger my solution, operations, or the company image?

☐ Does my timeline reflect all important milestones?

☐ Are the milestones realistic?

☐ Did I include an executive summary if my document is longer than seven pages?

☐ Is the writing clear and concise?

☐ Did I make my business case visually appealing?

Chapter 10

16 THOUGHTS ON DESIGNING POWERPOINT SLIDES

PowerPoint is a powerful graphics package from Microsoft that allows the user to easily produce professional quality slides, overhead transparencies, speaker's notes, and audience handouts on a personal computer. However, like all great tools, it can be abused and misused.

Used well, PowerPoint can give your presentation added impact. In addition, if you are nervous, it will take people's eyes off you. On the other hand, if overused, PowerPoint can confuse and bore audiences. It is usually the case that the more slides you use, the fewer questions are asked and the less transfer of learning takes place. The phrase "Death by PowerPoint" has become common.

I know of one teacher who says, "I use a lot of PowerPoint slides when I am not totally familiar with the material. As I become more comfortable, I start to delete or skip over slides." I pity the first few groups of students.

This chapter is not about improving the delivery of your presentation, but about making sure that the content of the slides is appropriate. Here are some guidelines:

1. Remember that you are not giving a PowerPoint presentation. You are giving a presentation using PowerPoint. Prepare your presentation first, and then decide where you need extra reinforcement for your ideas.

2. Understand the purpose of your presentation. Is it to inform, sell, or entertain? If you want to entertain or to give a "pep rally" speech, you can get fancy with flying bullets, builds, and fades — but don't overdo it. If you are trying to sell something, remember that you are not there to win an Oscar for special effects. You are there to win over audiences.

3. Decide where the slides fit best in your presentation.

    • Use slides to preview what material will be covered and to summarize what was covered.

    • Show slides with main points that you then expand on verbally or by using a flip chart.

    • Include pictures and drawings of things that are too complex to explain or to draw quickly on a flip chart.

4. Text on slides should be concise. Complete sentences don't work well. Keep to the "six-by-six rule." No more than six bullet points on a slide, with no more than six words per point. Separate points with white space.

    Example   (*text-heavy slide*)

    There are 4 common myths associated with business writing:

    • Sentences should never end with a preposition (e.g., *of, on,* or *to*).

    • You should never start a sentence with the words "and," "but," or "or."

    • You should use synonyms rather than repeating words.

    • As readers are busy, condense your material so that it fits onto one page.

Better

Successful Business Writers Ignore Myths:

- Never end with a preposition.
- Never start with *and, but,* or *or.*
- Never repeat words.
- Never write more than one page.

5. Don't read slides to your viewers. It insults their intelligence. They can normally read faster mentally. (It takes roughly eight seconds to silently read a typical slide of about 36 words.)

   A PowerPoint slide should be a framework for discussion. Ideally, you should show the slide, let the audience read it, and then elaborate on it yourself.

6. Too many slides with bullet points can be boring. Bullet points are best for lists and summaries. Use graphs, charts, and pictures for greater impact. By breaking up screens of words with visuals, you will help your reader to maintain his or her focus on your message. The eye picks up and the brain remembers pictures far better than words.

7. Use handout materials rather than PowerPoint slides to discuss detailed tables.

8. Use effective titles. Good titles sell a message; they don't just list what will be seen. This is particularly important if you are giving hard copy copies of your presentation to your audience. You want the sales message to shine through.

   Example (*poor title*)

   Lightweight, Aluminum Suitcases

   Better Make Your Business Trips Easier

9. Make sure you have plenty of contrast between the text color and the background color on a slide. Often, colors look fine on your computer monitor, but when they are projected, the colors alter. One recommended contrast combination is yellow or white text on a medium- to dark-blue background.

If you are presenting in a room that will be darkened, avoid using a black font on a white background. It is too hard on your audience's eyes.

Red text on a blue, black, or green background is impossible to see for people who are color blind.

10. Keep your font size to 24 points or bigger. Using 28 to 32 points is ideal. Titles stand out when they are at least 36 points.

11. Keep the fonts consistent throughout the presentation and use no more than two different fonts.

12. Proofread for grammar and spelling errors. Typos projected in front of an audience ruin a presenter's credibility.

13. Be cautious when inserting moving visuals. Anything that moves demands that the audience members use their time and energy to watch and to process the idea behind the visual. This distracts from the message. Moving text also forces the reader to wait until the text stops before it can be read, and forces the audience's attention on the screen and away from the presenter.

14. Choose your template carefully. Some templates have excessive branding (logos or company/department names) and copyright material on every slide. This makes it difficult for the readers to know what they are expected to read.

15. The number of PowerPoint slides you show should be based on the presentation time you have. If you have a whole day to work with a group, you could use up to 85 slides. If you have only an hour, don't use more than ten. If you have only five minutes, use only one slide with three main bullets and three subpoints.

16. If you want to demonstrate your competence, expertise, and belief in your message, engage your audience with stories, thought-provoking questions, and solid facts. Focus more on your personal delivery and your body language. Slides are visual aids. Use them for just that.

Use Checklist 8 to review the PowerPoint slides you have prepared.

CHECKLIST 8
POWERPOINT SLIDES

After you have prepared your talk and selected the PowerPoint slides, ask yourself:

☐ Did I choose my PowerPoint slides to aid my audience in understanding my message?

☐ Can I elaborate on the slides using stories, flip-chart drawings, handouts, or other support?

☐ Do the titles on the slides sell the message?

☐ Does my first slide explain what my talk will cover?

☐ Do the bulleted-list slides follow the six-by-six rule?

☐ Did I break up the bulleted-list slides with slides showing pictures or charts?

☐ Will the color on my slides work in the room where I will be presenting?

☐ Are the fonts consistent and large enough to be seen from the back of the room?

☐ Was I cautious about the amount of animation I added?

☐ Did I limit the number of slides to approximately ten per hour?

☐ Does my last slide summarize what I have presented?

Chapter 11
29 WAYS TO WRITE FOR THE WORLD WIDE WEB

In the twentieth century, the standard way to conduct business requiring written documentation was through letters, memos, and reports. In the late nineties, email messages were added to the list.

Now in the early twenty-first century, websites have become the latest mechanism to distribute information.

Business websites can carry items such as:

- Public relations messages
- Corporate mission statements
- Policies and procedures
- Human resources documentation
- Product information

There are three types of visitors to a corporate website: the divers, the skimmers, and the surfers. The divers are people who want detailed information and are prepared to spend the time to obtain it. Divers are quite happy to download long documents and read the information in print.

The skimmers want entertainment; the surfers want specific details — just the facts. Both skimmers and surfers want fast "hits" of information requiring little or no scrolling. Although skimmers are more prepared to watch "dancing baloney" — morphing, moving graphics — neither group will wait for long when having to download a message.

Therefore, there are two types of documents you can prepare for the web: archives and chunks.

Archived documents are ones that were initially prepared as print documents but are now being filed electronically. They often include graphics. These documents require a great deal of scrolling, so readers usually print them. Archived documents are great for policies and procedures, technical manuals, and annual reports. They are normally read only by the divers.

Skimmers and surfers prefer "chunked" documents: screen-sized passages of text that are usually no more than 100 words long. Every word is visible on the screen.

Some websites consist of both types of documents so as to satisfy the format preferences of all readers.

If you are preparing a document to be "archived" on a site, follow the rules listed earlier in this book. The following guidelines are focused on writing "chunk" documents for the web.

1. Research shows that reading from a screen takes 25 percent more time than reading from paper. (Even a top-range monitor cannot match the sharpness and detail of type on paper.) In addition, readers are much more likely to skim over a web page than to study it carefully. They are more impatient, concentrate less on detail, and are task driven. In other words, they scan pages looking for specific information and are quick to move to other sites when they are not entertained or when they cannot find required information easily.

2. The home page of your site should provide the reader with the following information:
    *   What the site is about
    *   How it is organized
    *   How to navigate it

3. Main titles should be capitalized and bolded. Skip beginning articles such as *the* or *a*. Make the first word an important, topic-carrying one. This will help search engines find your information faster.

   Weak　　　THE ROBOTICS INDUSTRY OF COBDEN

   Better　　ROBOTICS INDUSTRY OF COBDEN

4. As you can't guarantee readers will read the entire section before moving elsewhere, use a journalistic approach to organizing information: the inverted pyramid. Put the most important point first, then the second most important, then the third, and so on.

5. Each point should be chunked into sections consisting of approximately 100 words.

6. Each chunk should consist of two to three short paragraphs with a subhead. Paragraphs are usually three to five lines long.

7. Subheads should "talk." They should tell the reader what the section is about.

   Weak　　　Cobden's Robotics Industry

   Better　　Robotics Manufactured in Cobden Can Increase Your Productivity

8. Chunks should be surrounded by lots of white space to make them visually appealing.

9. The best line length for website reading is ten words per line (half the width of the screen).

10. Bullet lists work well on websites. Long sentences are too hard to read from a monitor.

11. If you are preparing a hard copy document that will later be reproduced as a chunked document on the screen, follow the writing techniques listed in Chapter 3. Then reduce it even more for the web document. Chunked documents should only be half as long as printed text; one-quarter would be even better.

12. Make your document look simple. Don't waste readers' time with information they don't need or want to know. If 80 percent of the readers won't need the information, then don't include it.

13. Adopt a "you" attitude. Web writing should put facts and ideas in terms of the reader's advantage. Be sure to talk more about the reader's needs than your own.

> **Example** Ontario's new wholesale electricity market provides equal, unbiased access to all generators, buyers, and sellers who are qualified to participate.

> **Better** If you qualify as a generator, buyer, or seller, you can access Ontario's new wholesale electricity market.

14. Web readers are busy. They dislike boastful writing or heavy commercialism. If you provide straight facts, you'll appear objective and trustworthy. Don't use a lot of adjectives. If you use a word such as *best*, make sure you document why your company is the *best* one in the market.

15. The most effective web pages are ones that were jointly prepared by both writers and designers from the beginning of the project. This is important because a good writer understands the reader's needs and can deliver the content of the message; a good designer excels at organizing this message so it is visually appealing. The content and the context must work together. If either stage gets ahead of the other, it may be time-consuming to back-track to make them match.

16. If it takes more than ten seconds to download a page, it is quite likely busy people will hit the stop button. Be careful with "dancing baloney" — moving graphics. If it takes your page longer to open, think twice. Although many designers like this feature, it often annoys busy readers.

17. Serif fonts are easier to read. (See Chapter 3, Rule 30.) Type size can range from 10 point to 14 point.

18. Use capital letters, small caps, italics, and boldface sparingly. Do not underline words because on the web an underline means a link.

19. Hyphenated words can make your screen look tidy, but the hyphens carry over to the print text where the line length may be different and will look like errors.

20. Don't use semicolons on a website. They are too hard to read on a monitor.

21. Page number references usually become meaningless when loading a document onto a site. So are the words *above mentioned* and *below mentioned*, unless you can guarantee the information referred to is in the next sentence.

22. Be consistent throughout the entire site in terms of navigation tools and words, tone, and style.

23. Color looks wonderful on a website, but some people equate blue text to "clickable" text (hypertext link), so never make text blue if it is not clickable. Similarly, avoid red or purple text, as these two colors are often used to show hypertext links that have already been accessed.

24. Don't distract your reader from your message with grammatical mistakes, typos, or misspellings. Writers often believe good grammar is not necessary in an email or on a website. However, readers are quick to notice errors, and the writer loses creditability.

25. Proofread online on different platforms and in different browsers. Check the text on a Mac and PC, in Internet Explorer, Netscape, and Firefox.

26. Never assume you know where your readers are coming from. Readers may be visiting your site from all over the world. If you are listing money amounts, make sure you include the currency and indicate if you will accept other currencies.

    US$5,000 CDN$5,000 £5,000*

---

*Although some countries are replacing commas with blank spaces when writing numbers, many banking institutions prefer to retain the commas to prevent the addition of extra numbers.

27. When providing measurements, include a conversion table or a link to a conversion site.

28. Be very specific when listing areas you will ship to. Don't just use cities or vague geographical references, such as *southwest*. Make sure you include states/provinces and countries.

    Poor   There are no shipping charges for any deliveries within a fifty mile radius.

    Better   There are no shipping charges for deliveries in the Greater Toronto (Canada) area.

29. Avoid words that may be foreign to your reader, such as jargon or local expressions.

    After you have edited your document for the web, take a look at Checklist 9.

CHECKLIST 9
WEBSITES

After you have prepared a document to be loaded onto a website, ask yourself:

☐ Did I determine who the main readers would be? Surfers or divers?

☐ Did I decide whether the readers would normally read the document in print form or on a computer screen?

☐ Is the first word in the main title an information-bearing word?

☐ Do the subheads tell a story?

☐ If the document was designed to be printed and read, did I follow the rules for clear, concise writing?

☐ If the article was designed to be read from the screen, did I ensure it was shorter than a similar print document?

☐ Is the information divided into easy-to-read chunks?

☐ Are lines and sentences short?

☐ Did I use lists to make information stand out?

☐ Is the document visually appealing on the screen?

☐ Is there consistency in navigation tools, words, and tone?

☐ Is the information free of grammar and spelling errors?

☐ Did I avoid hyphens, semicolons, and underlining?

☐ Did I clarify currencies and geographical locations for readers outside my country?

☐ Does the document download quickly?

Chapter 12

44 SUGGESTIONS TO WRITE FASTER, AVOID WRITER'S BLOCK, COACH OTHER WRITERS, AND BECOME AN EFFECTIVE GHOSTWRITER

This chapter consists of leftovers — the writing tips I have found helpful but which really don't fit into one specific spot. This is not to say that this information isn't important. In fact, most of these techniques can be used in handling any writing assignment.

WRITING FASTER

You've been given a writing assignment — a major report for your company, or an important letter — and you've developed a case of stage fright. You just can't get started, you can't focus your thoughts, and the words won't come. You despair of completing the assignment on time.

If so, the following section is especially for you. It helps you establish a writing routine and describes games to trick your mind over the hesitation.

1. I find writing is like holding a tangled ball of string in your hand. All the ideas, facts, questions, and answers are wrapped together, and you have to keep pulling and poking at them — designing purpose statements, working with

scratch pads, and preparing outlines — until everything suddenly unravels and the words pour forth. To try to start writing any earlier is a waste of time.

2. Select a good writing environment. Everyone requires something different. Some people can work only if they are surrounded by silence; others need noise or music. Some writers want to be able to stare out a window; others are happy only if their desks are completely clear of clutter. It doesn't matter; just determine what works for you.

3. Choose the appropriate tools or props. I have heard of one man who is more productive if he writes his reports standing up at a drafting table. A close friend has a hat she puts on when she wants to write. This is to remind herself and her colleagues that writing is the task she is concentrating on. A former coworker could work only if he had a large cup of coffee beside him. Have you identified your prop?

4. The time of day is important. We all have different body rhythms. This means we perform different tasks better at some times of the day than others. Many young people, who have been out of school for just a few years, claim their most productive writing time is late in the day. Older business people usually find their most productive time is first thing in the morning. Determine your best writing time and arrange your day so you work on important writing assignments during this period.

5. Set aside relatively large blocks of uninterrupted time in which to do your writing. Obviously one hour of uninterrupted time is better than three hours of interruptions. This suggestion is easy to follow if you have an office and can shut the door and turn off the phone, or if you have the luxury of working from home. However, if you are in an open office, you have a problem. The best I can suggest is to put a small sign in your workspace, stating that you are working on a report and asking not to be disturbed until a specific time. You can also notify your coworkers of this needed time-out.

6. When you receive a writing assignment, immediately organize your schedule to allow plenty of time for preparing, writing, rewriting, and editing. Leaving it too late means you won't have adequate time to perform all these tasks, and your report will not be as effective as it should be. Remember, again, the old tongue-in-cheek advice on how to eat an elephant — one bite at a time. Break the writing task into small, easy-to-digest steps.

    Also plan for adequate "simmering" time between the steps. This ensures you are continually examining the project with a relatively fresh eye.

7. Once you have identified the key points to be included in your report, you don't have to begin at the beginning and work your way straight through. You could begin at an easy section or a hard one. If you are waiting for research to be completed on one portion, begin writing another area.

8. Before writing, reread your notes and outline. Then take a break for a few minutes . Do something completely different for at least ten minutes. Come back and begin to write as fast as you can. Don't stop to edit or consult your notes. After you have finished the section, check your notes for any point you may have forgotten. Then edit for spelling, grammar, and visual appeal.

9. Do not write and edit at the same time. Too many business people start writing, and when they come to a word they're not happy with, they stop and check their thesaurus for a better one. Or if a sentence isn't perfect, they stop and rework it. This is wasting time.

    The different workings of the right and left sides of our brains are now common knowledge. The right brain handles the actual writing process. The left brain is responsible for spelling, grammar, and editing. When you pause to search for the best phrase or sentence, you halt the right brain's activities and let the left brain take over. What would happen if you tried to drive a car with your feet on the brake and the gas pedal at the same time? The ride would be jerky and your progress slow. Why operate your brain in this way? When you write and edit at the same time, you only slow yourself down.

Remember the golden rule for writers:

First write it; then make it right.

10. If you have to stop before you have finished the entire writing phase — because the project is too long to complete in that sitting, or because it is time to go to a meeting or lunch or home — be careful where you leave off. If you complete an entire section, when you come back to write you will have to reread much of the previous material before you can get started. However, if you quit in the middle of a sentence in the middle of a paragraph in the middle of a section, you'll find it easier to resume writing in the future. Just reread the sentence and fill in the missing information. This should lead you into the next sentence and so forth. This is a very simple, effective technique, but it is surprisingly hard to do.

11. Another technique, if you have to call it a day before finishing the project, is to leave yourself notes for the next day's work.

12. Divide the editing stage into three phases. First, review the material to determine if all the important details have been included or if any points need further explanation. Second, check the material for style, grammar, spelling, and punctuation. Third, look at the appearance. Is there plenty of white space? Does it look easy to read?

13. Read your draft aloud. Put a pencil check wherever you stumble, but don't stop reading. When you have finished, go back to the marked sections. These are the areas you have to improve.

14. Some people can go for weeks in their jobs and not have to write anything more than a few short emails. Keep your writing "muscles" in shape. Read and edit everything you can get your hands on. It will prepare you for your next writing challenge.

15. Maintain a file of correspondence and reports you think are particularly well written. These documents may serve as future references for layout and organization.

16. The best way to become a good writer is to write and write and write.

AVOIDING WRITER'S BLOCK

Sometimes, no matter how hard you push, the words and ideas just won't come. This happens to all writers at some point. Here are some ideas to break through the barrier.

17. Let it go. Move away from the keyboard and do something else, preferably something that doesn't involve creative thinking. Make some sales calls, organize your desk or files, make photocopies, or run errands. After a minimum of one hour — preferably two — turn back to the keyboard and the ideas should flow. Your brain has had a chance to recharge.

18. Write a letter. Take the details you are wrestling with and explain them in a letter to a close friend.

19. Imagine you are talking on the phone. How would you explain this important message to the listener?

20. Start with a purpose sentence. Begin by writing *The purpose of this (letter, memo, or report) is to …* and then add *why*.

21. Open a dictionary at random and choose a word. Use this word in the first sentence in your document.

22. Write badly and then leave the material for a day. Hopefully, you will find something salvageable in it when you come back to it.

23. Try writing with colored markers on legal-size paper, or on paper that is even larger.

24. Dictate your thoughts into a tape recorder.

25. Don't edit and write at the same time (see Rule 9).

26. Relax. This, of course, is easier for people working at home. Meditate. Read a book. Perform some deep breathing exercises.

27. Get some exercise. Go for a walk; play a game of squash or racquetball. This remedy is often the most effective. It chases away the cobwebs, gets the blood flowing, and releases creative energies.

HELPING OTHERS IMPROVE THEIR WRITING

Helping others improve their writing is not an easy task. If you continually make major revisions to your employees' work, chances are they will give up trying to improve. "After all, why bother?" they'll say. "The boss will only rewrite it."

On the other hand, if you overlook vague or poorly written correspondence, it will reflect badly on your department and organization.

Here are some guidelines to help you coach your staff in preparing well-written documents.

28. First, ensure your own writing reflects today's business writing style: clear, concise, and courteous.

29. Establish a sense of ownership. Assign projects to be written and allow people to work on them.

30. Discuss projects thoroughly and come to an agreement early on regarding the direction of the project and deadlines.

31. Understand the differences between editing, rewriting, and revising. If you are editing, your job is to improve the clarity, accuracy, and effectiveness of the material. The changes are minor, and you could make the alterations without consulting the author.

    When you revise, you indicate the changes required in the sentence structure, tone, organization, and the inclusion or elimination of details. Then you pass it back to the author so he or she can rewrite the material. This is a good learning process for the author but can be time-consuming.

    Rewriting is when you make the changes yourself instead of letting the author make them. This is faster, but the writer will not learn from the experience.

32. Don't attempt to edit someone else's work when you are in a bad mood. When you are angry or upset, your judgment is off and you will end up revising material that at another time would be acceptable.

33. Choose a comprehensive style and grammar book that is available to everyone in the office.

34. Don't use a red pen when correcting someone's work. It makes people feel they are back in school.

35. Change words only if they are incorrect or fuzzy. Don't change words because they aren't your favorite words.

36. Never rewrite an entire paragraph. Mark it for the author to revise.

37. Don't write cryptic words, such as *confusing* or *awkward*, in the margin. Comment on why the passage isn't working.

38. If a problem appears repeatedly, number your comments and refer to the number when the problem appears again, rather than rewriting your concerns.

39. Circulate well-written reports so staff have a standard to go by.

40. Praise your staff — preferably in public — whenever they prepare a well-written document.

BEING A GHOSTWRITER

Being asked to write a letter or memo for someone else (who will put his or her signature on it) is not uncommon in the business world. Perhaps the person you are writing for is busy, or perhaps you have more background or insight into the situation than he or she does. In any case, ghostwriting can be tricky. "Signers" want documents to match their own writing styles.

41. After you have considered the reader and the details to be included, analyze the signer's normal writing style and then temporarily adopt it.

    Does the signer:

    • Begin with a pompous opening or a reference to the reader?

- Use a friendly or pompous note?
- Favor the pronoun: *I, you, we,* or *it?*
- Arrange series of ideas in lists?
- Prefer long or short paragraphs and sentences?
- Have any favorite words?
- Use the active voice more than the passive voice?
- Use contractions such as *it's* and *can't,* or spell words out in full?
- Close with a refreshing ending or a cliché?

42. The signer's personality usually shows more in the beginning and end than in the body, so match the signer's normal opening and closing lines as much as possible.

43. Do not be upset when, after you have worked hard to adopt the signer's style, he or she still makes changes. This is to be expected. Most signers feel they must make some alteration to the document in order to claim some authorship.

    However, do not complete ghostwriting assignments in a careless manner because you expect signers to revise them. This will only make you look incapable and unprofessional.

44. If a signer's style is completely outdated, you are not going to be able to change him or her overnight. You are going to have to compromise. Hopefully, you will find a middle-of-the-road style you both can live with.